CRAIG GROESCHEL

WITH DUDLEY DELFFS

LEAD LIKE IT MATTERS

WORKBOOK

7 Leadership Principles for a Church That Lasts

Harper*Christian*
Resources

Lead Like It Matters Workbook
© 2022 by Craig Groeschel

Requests for information should be addressed to:
HarperChristian Resources, 3900 Sparks Dr. SE, Grand Rapids, Michigan 49546

ISBN 978-0-310-15121-0 (softcover)
ISBN 978-0-310-15135-7 (ebook)

HarperChristian Resources titles may be purchased in bulk for church, business, fundraising, or ministry use. For information, please e-mail ResourceSpecialist@ChurchSource.com.

Published in association with Winters & King, Inc.

First Printing August 2022 / Printed in the United States of America

Contents

Introduction

Some ministries have *it*. Some don't.

Most churches want *it*. Few have it.

When a church has *it*, everyone knows it. When one doesn't—well, everyone knows that too.

The same is true with pastors and leaders. Some have *it*. Some don't. It is obvious when someone has *it* and when someone doesn't.

It is always unique. It is always powerful. It is always life-changing.

So . . . what is *it*?

My answer is . . . I don't know. Really, I don't.

It is hard to define because you can't see it. But here's what I do know: If you've ever been involved in a ministry that had *it*, you had this sense you were part of something special. Although you probably couldn't describe *it*, you still knew it when you saw it. It was an indescribable work of God that could not be explained or contained.

If you've never seen *it* up close, ask around and see if you can find it. Just listen to what people around you are saying. I promise, if a ministry or church near you gets *it*, people will be talking about it. When a ministry has *it*, there's electricity in the air; the ground seems to rumble. Everyone becomes aware of it. You'll see it on social media. People will talk about it at the office. Your friends will tell you they heard about it from their friends.

Because of the buzz, people flock to check out churches that have *it*. Not only do they kick the tires, but many of them also join. Not only do they join, but many also get obsessed with the ministry and throw their whole hearts and lives into it. They seem to intuitively grasp whatever *it* is. They can't get enough of it.

Here is something else I know: while *it* is always and only a gift from God, I believe that he makes *it* available to anyone who wants it. I believe that he wants to give *it* to you and your ministry. In whatever capacity you serve, you can learn to lead like *it* matters.

In this workbook, we will dive into the concepts that I present in the *Lead Like It Matters* book. Here's the game plan. In part 1, we'll talk about what *it* is and why we need to lead like it matters. In part 2, we'll explore seven leadership principles for building a church, ministry, or organization that lasts. In part 3, we'll discuss three important realms of leadership that every church or ministry leader must master to lead like *it* matters and maximize their God-given potential.

If you believe God wants to use you in his church and as his church, this study is for you. As you read on, do so prayerfully. If possible, don't go through this material alone. Invite friends from your small group, staff, or church leadership team to join you. Finally, be sure to keep an open mind, be alert to God's prompting, and believe by faith that he will hear the cries of your heart and move freely and powerfully through your church and ministry.

NOTE

This workbook is a biblical approach to practical leadership. For your convenience, in the following pages, you will find significant portions from the book *Lead Like It Matters*. The segments from the book are provided for you in this workbook so that you don't have to flip back and forth between the workbook and the book. In the following pages, you will also find additional biblical application to support the leadership content, to enable you to lead a church that lasts, and discussion questions to cover with your team.

PART 1

WHAT IS *IT*?

When God gives it to you,
it is unmistakable.

Depending on your church background, you likely think some things are necessary to have a great church worship experience. Whatever you think you need, though, we didn't have that when we started Life.Church.

We didn't have a nice building. We didn't have our own offices. We didn't have a church phone number (unless you count my home phone number). We didn't have a paid staff. We didn't have a logo. We didn't have a website. We didn't serve Starbucks. We didn't have an organ. We didn't have a choir with robes or a rock band with guys wearing skinny jeans and sporting lots of hair product. We didn't have candles to spark the mood or a laser light show that pierced through the smoke from the fog machines. We didn't have hymnals or sermon series with titles copied from the most popular TV shows.

What did we have? We had a few people, but those few people were off-the-charts excited about Jesus. We had enough Bibles to go around. And we had *it*.

At the time, I didn't call it *it*.

But we were definitely full of *it*.

Even though we didn't know what *it* was, we knew it was from God. And it was special.

Whatever *it* was, everyone felt it. They talked about it. New people came and experienced it. The church grew. And grew. And grew. Lives were changed by the dozens. Then by the hundreds. Then by the thousands. Twenty-five years later, we are known as the largest attended church in the history of North America.

God's Word Has *It*

You can find *it* in all types of churches. It is in traditional churches, contemporary churches, charismatic churches, seeker-sensitive churches, and emergent churches. You can find it in rural communities, in suburbs, in big cities, and in underground churches in countries where it's illegal to meet for corporate worship.

Even though you can find *it* in all of those places, you can also go to thousands of these same types of churches that don't have it.

But when God gives *it* to you, it is unmistakable.

And when a ministry has *it*, most things the leaders try seem to work.

When a ministry has *it*, the staff knows they're part of something much bigger than themselves. They are important players participating in a divine mission, an unstoppable force, flowing with contagious passion. They show up early for almost everything. They often stay late. They rarely fight. When they do disagree, they grow through their differences, usually quickly.

When a church has *it*, creativity flows. Everyone comes up with ideas, and those ideas just seem to change lives.

On the other hand, when a ministry doesn't have *it*, most of what they try doesn't work. A ministry that doesn't have *it* simply follows the same formula they used the year before and the year before that. People are bored, uninspired, and complacent.

When a church doesn't have *it*, the staff is simply doing a job, drawing a paycheck, passing time. They're territorial. Jealous. Dissatisfied. Discontented. Even bitter.

When a church doesn't have *it*, few people seem to even notice. They don't seem to realize that no one new is showing up. It's certainly not a cause for alarm. Mostly they're just committed to and comfortable with the status quo.

When a church does have *it*, everyone knows it. They can feel it, though they would have trouble describing it. Everyone recognizes it, but no one knows precisely what it is.

It's a lot like the first-century church you read about in the book of Acts. They unquestionably had *it.* Look for *it* in this description of the early church and then answer the questions that follow.

> [42] They devoted themselves to the apostles' teaching and to fellowship, to the breaking of bread and to prayer. [43] Everyone was filled with awe at the many wonders and signs performed by the apostles. [44] All the believers were together and had everything in common. [45] They sold property and possessions to give to anyone who had need. [46] Every day they continued to meet together in the temple courts. They broke bread in their homes and ate together with glad and sincere hearts, [47] praising God and enjoying the favor of all the people. And the Lord added to their number daily those who were being saved.
>
> **—Acts 2:42–47**

_____

■ Based on this passage, what are some key elements necessary for a church to have *it?* How have you experienced these elements in your church today?

■ Knowing that the early church contained both Jews and Gentiles, both free people and slaves, both men and women (see Galatians 3:28), what does it means that "all the believers were together and had everything in common"?

■ In what ways did the attitudes of believers have an impact on the early church? In your experience, what has the greatest influence on the attitudes of church members?

■ Why do you think the early church attracted others who came to know the Lord? How did the early church reflect the qualities and characteristics of Jesus?

They Got *It*

You can lead like *it* matters, but you can't create it. How might leaders try to do that? Someone might visit a growing church and observe outward signs of success—videos, buildings, fancy kids' rooms, a certain style of music, and so on. These well-meaning guests mistakenly think, *That's why they have it. If we had all that, we'd have it too.*

They couldn't be more wrong.

The first-century church in Jerusalem clearly had *it*. Yet they didn't have anything extravagant. No historic cathedrals. No professionally produced video roll-ins to the latest four-part sermon series. No climbing walls in the youth wing or LED wall in the auditorium.

So, *it* can't possibly be stained-glass windows, hand-carved cherubs, custom silk tapestries, gold-inlaid hymnals, thousand-pipe organs, marble floors, mile-high steeples, hand-painted ceilings, mahogany pews, giant cast-iron bells, and a three-piece, thousand-dollar suit. *It* doesn't stick any better to a young, hip pastor with tattoos and overpriced kicks than it does to an older, stately gentleman in a robe.

Nor is *it* spotlights and lasers, video production, satellite dishes, fog machines, shiny gauze backdrops, four-color glossy brochures, creative billboards, loud "contemporary" music, free donuts, coffee shops, hip bookstores, break dancing or acrobatics, sermon series based on movies, or a retro-modern matching chair and table onstage. It is not being on television, streaming on YouTube, speaking at conferences, having your own leadership podcast, or doing Instagram Live with the hottest celebrities.

What is *it* and how do you get it? I don't know. But God does. And I think he would tell you it's not one thing; it's the right combination of some essential ingredients. You can develop it from the recipe he's handed down, generation to generation, from those first Christians we read about in the book of Acts.

> [31] After they prayed, the place where they were meeting was shaken. And they were all filled with the Holy Spirit and spoke the word of God boldly.
>
> [32] All the believers were one in heart and mind. No one claimed that any of their possessions was their own, but they shared everything they had. [33] With great power the apostles continued to testify to the resurrection of the Lord Jesus. And God's grace was so powerfully at work in them all [34] that there were no needy persons among them. For from time to time those who owned land or houses sold them, brought the money from the sales [35] and put it at the apostles' feet, and it was distributed to anyone who had need.
>
> **—Acts 4:31–35**

_____

■ What stands out to you in this description of the early church? Why?

■ What *it*-qualities, both for a leader and a church, emerge from this passage? How have you seen these qualities manifest in churches where you've served?

■ How did the Holy Spirit empower and facilitate *it* in the believers of the early church? What's the Spirit's role as you pursue leading like it matters?

■ When have you experienced God's grace "powerfully at work" in you and your ministry? What did you learn about *it* from that experience?

Factoring *It* In

Part of what makes it *it* is that it defies categorization. It won't reduce to a memorable slogan or catchy formula. It is far too special for that.

That's why we have to embrace the fact that God makes *it* happen. It is from him. It is by him. It is for his glory. We can't create it. We can't reproduce it. We can't manufacture it.

It is not a model. It is not a style. It is not the result of a program. You can't purchase it or assemble it. It can't be copied.

Not everyone will get *it*. It can't be learned in a classroom. Yet even though it can't be taught, it *can* be caught.

As you begin considering what *it* is and where it comes from, remember:

- Beautiful buildings, cool environments, and the right technology aren't necessary to have *it*.
- A person surrendered fully to Christ gets *it*.
- Once a person has *it*, he can't keep it to himself.
- The good news: if you don't have *it*, you can get it.
- The bad news: if you have *it*, you can lose it.
- *It* is not a model, system, or result of programs.
- You cannot purchase *it*. It can't be copied.
- Not everyone will get *it*.
- *It* cannot be learned. Even though it can't be taught, it can be caught.
- *It* happens when we allow God to grow certain vital characteristics in us and in the ministries we lead.

- Have you ever been part of a ministry or organization that had *it?* What were some of the qualities that you experienced and appreciated?

- Do you agree or disagree that *it* can be found in all types of churches? Why? What's the basis for your answer?

- Sometimes you can identify *it* by what it isn't. What comes to mind when you consider describing what *it* isn't?

- When have you tried to add or subtract something in your ministry in order to get *it?* What were your results?

Putting *It* into Action

You may feel challenged, frustrated, confused, and overwhelmed as you begin experiencing *it* and putting *it* into action in your ministry. And you may also feel excited, intrigued, exhilarated, and connected to God and others like never before. As you prepare to examine the various elements contributing to *it* in Part 2 of this workbook, think about how you would define *it* based on your own experience. Use the questions below to help you consider what you already know about *it* and where you're already seeing God using it in your life and work.

■ Based on your observations and experiences, as well as what you see in God's Word, how would you define *it* in a sentence or two? How do you think members of your team would define it?

■ What are the strongest areas in your church or organization, the places where you see *it* making an impact? What areas are struggling and lacking in *it?*

■ How do the seven key ingredients listed below work together to reflect Christ and advance God's kingdom? While you will examine each one in more detail in Part 2, write down your initial thoughts about how each ingredient contributes to *it* based on your experience and observations.

Vision:

Divine Focus:

Unmistakable Camaraderie:

Innovative Minds:

Willingness to Fall Short:

Hearts Focused Outward:

Kingdom-Mindedness:

- Finally, based on what we've covered so far, what stands out most to you? What's required for you to lead like it matters? Contact a close, trusted friend or colleague and share your answers to these two questions.

PART 2

WHAT CONTRIBUTES TO *IT*?

Vision

Without a God-given vision, our ministries
will never get it *or keep* it.

N ot every church can achieve *it* the same way. They'd be foolish to try. Not every church will have a charismatic preacher or a well-known worship pastor. Not every church can afford a nice building. Not every church can bus in hundreds of kids to their youth ministry or host a large vacation Bible school. Not every church can have sermon clips go viral or have thousands of downloads on YouTube.

No two churches achieve *it* the same way. But I've found that churches that have *it* do have some consistent qualities. The first of these qualities is vision.

If you want to lead like it matters, vision is essential. And not just having a vision, but casting it, sharing it, bringing it to life, and updating it as God leads. Churches and ministries that have *it* always have a clear vision. The people know, understand, believe, and live out the vision. The vision guides, motivates, energizes, and compels them. Large numbers of people passionately move in the same direction. They know it's not simply the leader's vision—it's God's vision for them as his people. In other words, it's a shared vision.

The Bible couldn't be clearer on the necessity of this key ingredient: "Where there is no vision, the people perish" (Proverbs 29:18 KJV). Without direction, people drift. Without a goal, motivation wanes. Without a mission, ministries fade. Youth groups lose their life. Once-vibrant churches slowly die. We need a clear and compelling vision that is constantly and enthusiastically cast.

People in a visionless church are often busy doing activities without any clear idea of how they relate or fulfill a larger purpose. They're moving in place without going toward a destination. Without a compelling vision, people quickly wear themselves out from all the activities and busyness. Those who frequently serve burn out. Staff members grow frustrated. Boards, elders, deacons, and leaders often disagree and split into factions. The ministry may have tons of activity, but there's little spiritual movement. Without alignment between the vision and the movement, they crash.

Vision matters to God and to those who serve him: "And the Lord answered me and said, Write the vision and engrave it so plainly upon tablets that everyone who passes may [be able to] read [it easily and quickly] as he hastens by" (Habakkuk 2:2 AMPC). Other translations say this vision is supposed to be carried by a "runner" or a "herald," and it should be so clear, displayed so prominently, that people can see it and read it at a glance.

With a known and implemented vision, you have clarity, focus, and direction. A white-hot vision inspires generosity, motivates selflessness, and releases an unstoppable passion to honor God and serve people. A vision empowers a church to have *it*.

Leaders who want vision seek God, find a divine burden, examine their resources and context, and present a Spirit-breathed, God-sized vision! As a leader, this is your role. This certainly doesn't mean that you won't listen to people, seeking their wisdom and input. But ultimately, the vision comes from the leader's time of hearing from God.

Don't assume you're not responsible for casting a God-given vision because you're not in a formal leadership role. When we follow Christ, we are all leaders. Because, at its core, what is leadership? Leadership is influence. Whether or not you have a title, your role, gifts, and contribution always matter in God's church. You always have influence—so use it!

As God gives you clarity, you'll want to work hard to communicate this vision. A powerful vision is memorable, portable, and motivational. If people can't remember your vision, your church will never have *it*. If your vision isn't concise and easy to grasp and implement, people will not buy in and feel part of it. If your vision doesn't stir people and move them to action, your vision is too small. Your vision must be something that burns in your heart but is too big for you to do on your own. If you could do it, you wouldn't need God.

If you want to lead like it matters, then never underestimate vision.

God's Word Has *It*

When a leader and a church share a vision, everyone knows it. They can feel it, though they might have trouble describing it. Everyone recognizes *it*, but no one knows precisely what it is. We see *it* clearly in the first-century church described in the book of Acts. Peter, a follower of Jesus not particularly known to be a dynamic leader—in fact, just the opposite—managed to share Christ's vision for what this community of believers could be. Shortly after receiving the Holy Spirit at Pentecost (see Acts 2:1–4), these followers of Jesus began to speak through the power of the Spirit—yet each could understand one another in their own native language. They were so amazed and bewildered by this experience that others around them began to assume they were drunk on wine (see verse 13).

Peter seized the opportunity to preach, and not only did his words convey the essence of the gospel of Jesus Christ to a largely Jewish crowd, but his sermon also ignited a vision of who Jesus was and consequently who they were as his followers. Read through the following excerpt from Peter's sermon and then answer the questions that follow.

[29] "Fellow Israelites, I can tell you confidently that the patriarch David died and was buried, and his tomb is here to this day. [30] But he was a prophet and knew that God had promised him on oath that he would place one of his descendants on his throne. [31] Seeing what was to come, he spoke of the resurrection of the Messiah, that he was not abandoned to the realm of the dead, nor did his body see decay. [32] God has raised this Jesus to life, and we are all witnesses of it. [33] Exalted to the right hand of God, he has received from the Father the promised Holy Spirit and has poured out what you now see and hear. [34] For David did not ascend to heaven, and yet he said,

"'The Lord said to my Lord:
        "Sit at my right hand
[35] until I make your enemies
        a footstool for your feet."'

[36] "Therefore let all Israel be assured of this: God has made this Jesus, whom you crucified, both Lord and Messiah."

[37] When the people heard this, they were cut to the heart and said to Peter and the other apostles, "Brothers, what shall we do?"

[38] Peter replied, "Repent and be baptized, every one of you, in the name of Jesus Christ for the forgiveness of your sins. And you will receive the gift of the Holy Spirit. [39] The promise is for you and your children and for all who are far off—for all whom the Lord our God will call."

[40] With many other words he warned them; and he pleaded with them, "Save yourselves from this corrupt generation." [41] Those who accepted his

message were baptized, and about three thousand were added to their number that day.

⁴² They devoted themselves to the apostles' teaching and to fellowship, to the breaking of bread and to prayer. ⁴³ Everyone was filled with awe at the many wonders and signs performed by the apostles. ⁴⁴ All the believers were together and had everything in common. ⁴⁵ They sold property and possessions to give to anyone who had need. ⁴⁶ Every day they continued to meet together in the temple courts. They broke bread in their homes and ate together with glad and sincere hearts, ⁴⁷ praising God and enjoying the favor of all the people. And the Lord added to their number daily those who were being saved.

—Acts 2:29–47

■ How did Peter help his listeners, many of whom were likely resistant to accepting Jesus as the Messiah, accept Christ and his sacrifice on the cross? In other words, how did Peter share a new vision of how they saw Jesus?

■ Why do you think Peter mentioned David's tomb before transitioning to Christ's resurrection? Why did Peter quote David from one of the Psalms (110:1)?

■ What impact did Peter's sermon have on those listening? Why did they ask, "What shall we do?" (Acts 2:37)?

■ What evidence is provided at the end of this passage that this church had *it?* How did they put their vision of Christ into action?

They Got *It*

The seven ingredients that reflect *it* don't just emerge from contemporary leaders and churches—we find plenty of examples throughout the Bible. While numerous people in Scripture demonstrate vision, one in particular reveals how crucial it is to get everyone on board to see the vision realized. Nehemiah, part of the exiled remnant of Jewish people still in Babylon, served as cupbearer to King Artaxerxes, a role of honor reflecting Nehemiah's integrity. Although he wasn't a priest, prophet, or scribe, Nehemiah used his influence to initiate change and follow through.

After two groups of Jews had returned to Israel, word apparently got back to those remaining in Babylon about what they found. Basically, their homeland was in ruins. The walls around Jerusalem had fallen, leaving the city vulnerable to thieves and vandals. When Nehemiah heard the news, he mourned the loss, but he also trusted God to carry out Jerusalem's restoration. Read the following passage describing Nehemiah's vision quest, and then answer the questions that follow.

¹ In the month of Nisan in the twentieth year of King Artaxerxes, when wine was brought for him, I took the wine and gave it to the king. I had not been sad in his presence before, ² so the king asked me, "Why does your face look so sad when you are not ill? This can be nothing but sadness of heart."

I was very much afraid, ³ but I said to the king, "May the king live forever! Why should my face not look sad when the city where my ancestors are buried lies in ruins, and its gates have been destroyed by fire?"

⁴ The king said to me, "What is it you want?"

Then I prayed to the God of heaven, ⁵ and I answered the king, "If it pleases the king and if your servant has found favor in his sight, let him send me to the city in Judah where my ancestors are buried so that I can rebuild it."

⁶ Then the king, with the queen sitting beside him, asked me, "How long will your journey take, and when will you get back?" It pleased the king to send me; so I set a time.

⁷ I also said to him, "If it pleases the king, may I have letters to the governors of Trans-Euphrates, so that they will provide me safe-conduct until I arrive in Judah? ⁸ And may I have a letter to Asaph, keeper of the royal park, so he will give me timber to make beams for the gates of the citadel by the temple and for the city wall and for the residence I will occupy?" And because the gracious hand of my God was on me, the king granted my requests. ⁹ So I went to the governors of Trans-Euphrates and gave them the king's letters. The king had also sent army officers and cavalry with me.

¹⁰ When Sanballat the Horonite and Tobiah the Ammonite official heard about this, they were very much disturbed that someone had come to promote the welfare of the Israelites.

¹¹ I went to Jerusalem, and after staying there three days ¹² I set out during the night with a few others. I had not told anyone what my God had put in my heart to do for Jerusalem. There were no mounts with me except the one I was riding on.

[13] By night I went out through the Valley Gate toward the Jackal Well and the Dung Gate, examining the walls of Jerusalem, which had been broken down, and its gates, which had been destroyed by fire. [14] Then I moved on toward the Fountain Gate and the King's Pool, but there was not enough room for my mount to get through; [15] so I went up the valley by night, examining the wall. Finally, I turned back and reentered through the Valley Gate. [16] The officials did not know where I had gone or what I was doing, because as yet I had said nothing to the Jews or the priests or nobles or officials or any others who would be doing the work.

[17] Then I said to them, "You see the trouble we are in: Jerusalem lies in ruins, and its gates have been burned with fire. Come, let us rebuild the wall of Jerusalem, and we will no longer be in disgrace." [18] I also told them about the gracious hand of my God on me and what the king had said to me.

They replied, "Let us start rebuilding." So they began this good work.

—Nehemiah 2:1–18

_____

- What's striking about the fact that the king asked Nehemiah, his cupbearer, why he was sad? What does their exchange reveal about the kind of relationship they had?

- What are the main pieces required to fulfill Nehemiah's vision of a restored Jerusalem? How does he go about getting others to help him make these pieces fall into place?

■ What obstacles did Nehemiah face in the pursuit of fulfilling his vision? How did he handle them?

■ How does Nehemiah rely on God rather than his own abilities to execute his vision for rebuilding Jerusalem? What difference does this make in how he interacts with those around him?

Factoring *It* In

Though people may drift toward comfort and complacency, they don't really like it. Deep down, they desire more—a lot more. Everyone craves a cause worth fighting for. We want to feel like our lives are significant and have purpose. We love to be part of something bigger than ourselves, something making a real, even an eternal, difference. As leaders, it's our role to seek God, see the vision, communicate it in a compelling way, and invite people to give their lives for the greatest cause on earth—the cause of Christ.

When it comes to vision, remember:

- Without a vision, the people will never get *it* and keep *it*.
- Without a compelling vision, staff and volunteers get frustrated, disagree, and burn out.

- *It* doesn't show up on its own. *It* follows big vision.
- The vision must be memorable, portable, and motivational.
- You can't overcommunicate vision!
- People give sacrificially toward, tolerate inconveniences for, and love to share a compelling vision.

Now spend a few minutes considering your leadership tendencies as they relate to vision. Be as openhanded and clear-eyed as possible when considering the role vision has played in the ways you lead. Use these questions to help you clarify and improve your God-given vision and how you implement it.

———————————————————————

- What's one area of your ministry that's currently struggling because of lack of vision? How can you tell this area needs a clearer, sharper vision? Commit to praying about the vision God wants you to share so that this area really has *it*.

- As concisely and accurately as possible, write down your current vision statement for ministry:

■ Now evaluate your vision statement in regard to the three criteria below. For each one, give yourself a score between 1 to 10, with 1 being "needs help" and 10 being "just like Jesus."

Memorable: _____
Portable: _____
Motivational: _____

■ Think through how you can sharpen your vision statement to raise your score for each of these criteria. How can you seek God and cast a clear vision that others can embrace and execute?

Putting *It* into Action

Ministries that have *it* are filled with people who understand and believe in the vision. Without it, you will have people who like the ministry but don't understand—or care—where it's going. Generally, people fall into three levels of vision buy-in. Some believe in the vision enough to benefit from it. These are often people who attend church with a consumer mindset, expecting only to receive something or benefit from the ministry. They want to know there's a vision but don't feel personally compelled to invest in it.

Others believe in it enough to contribute comfortably to it. They have likely shifted from the casual first level to a place where they want to contribute if it's not inconvenient or too costly. These individuals like being part of the cause as long as it fits in with the rest of their lives.

Ideally, more and more people believe in the vision enough to give their lives to it. They understand it and get it. They want to serve a cause greater than themselves. They love Jesus and consider themselves merely stewards of all the resources—time, money, energy, relationships—in their lives. They don't look for what church can do for them but know they *are* the church. They're all in and totally get it.

With these three groups in mind, think about the people who participate in your church, ministry, or organization. Then answer the questions below and consider what your responses reveal about how you can increase buy-in for the vision God has given you.

■ Approximately what percentage of participants fall into each group?

Level 1: _____ %
Level 2: _____ %
Level 3: _____ %

■ How do you imagine the people in each group grasp your ministry's vision? How many of them would be able to express this vision?

———————————————————

Now spend a few moments praying about your relationships with these people. Ask God to show you how to communicate, connect, and care about them just as much as he does. Then choose one individual from each category and reach out to them this week. Let them know you're refining and clarifying your vision for ministry and would like their input.

PRINCIPLE #2

Divine Focus

To be great at a few things and experience it,
you'll have to say no to many things.

The second ingredient in churches and organizations that have *it* may seem obvious: *divine focus*. After all, if Jesus is the hope of the world—and he is—then the church, as the body of Christ, exists to serve others as his hands and feet, showing them the love of God in action. As his church, we are chosen and called by God to be light in the darkness and to give hope to those in despair. We are God's conduits of grace to a world of people who need him. Which is why *it* matters!

The problem with having a divine focus is that, filtered through you, your team, and those in your care, that focus tends to sprawl. Divine focus through human filters can become an ever-increasing list of new methods, new ministries, and misplaced resources. Because doing more requires allocating more—more time and money, more staff and volunteers, more resources and energy.

Most ministries that have *it*, however, tend to be focused on a limited set of targets. They do a few things as if all eternity hinged on their results, and they do these things with godly excellence. They clearly see the vision and drive toward it with laser-guided precision. Those who have *it* know what they are called to do. Perhaps just as important (maybe even more so), they also know what they are *not* called to do. Their vision is characterized by three things.

Specificity. Selectivity. Exclusivity.

Of course, focused ministries don't necessarily see immediate and overwhelming results. It often takes time, patience, discipline, and endurance. Then gradually they begin to realize that God is doing something special in their midst—they have *it.*

These churches remain relentlessly passionate about a few important things. They choose to deliberately ignore the rest. Their zeal and effectiveness attract the right leaders. The right leaders use their gifts and give their lives to make a difference. And God blesses them and their endeavors with *it*—his mysteriously awesome presence and power.

Unfortunately, when a ministry is faithful and one day wakes up and has *it,* they can be blinded by their success. Instead of seeing with the crystal clear vision that helped attract *it,* they find their vision begins to become blurred. Instead of staying focused on the main thing, the leaders become distracted by doing more and more. Sadly, the very thing that God blessed—strategic obedience to his specific calling—is one of the first things successful ministries unknowingly abandon.

The process of diluting divine focus usually happens subtly or covertly. Someone has a good idea that gets accepted and implemented—but the problem is that it's not a *God* idea. Someone's good idea sounded logical, reasonable, and feasible at the time, the natural progression of your ministry's growth. But it pulled focus away from God and what your ministry is called to do.

Rather than doing lots of things halfway, divine focus requires directing energy and resources at your God-given target with laser intensity. Because doing the wrong new things, things that usurp what God calls you to do, is dangerous. Focus tends to let *it* breathe. Lack of focus generally suffocates *it.*

To be great at a few things and experience *it,* you'll have to say no to many things. Instead of thinking about what you want to add to your ministry to-do list, maybe you should pray about what to add to your ministry to-*don't* list. Some call it planned abandonment—planning what things you *won't* do, that others do, in order to do best what God called you to do.

Most people think you achieve more by doing more. As counterintuitive as it sounds, you actually achieve a greater impact by doing less. If you say "yes" to too many different things, you lose focus and effectiveness. That's why you strategically and ruthlessly must say no. You don't grow by saying yes to everything. You grow by saying no.

Those who have *it* stick with what brings it. When you know you're doing a great work, do your best not to get distracted. If you have *it*, guard it. Don't distort it by doing the wrong things. When you increase your focus, you decrease your options. Good things are not necessarily God things.

Focus on what God has uniquely called and equipped you and your church to do. And then do it with excellence for his glory and his kingdom.

God's Word Has *It*

In order to rely on a divine focus, you must rely on the Divine. Your ability to infuse your leadership with *it*—the amazing power and presence of God's Spirit—depends on the quality of your personal relationship with God. Your example should inspire and motivate those you lead and serve to make their personal relationship with him their priority as well. Your ministry team must be plugged into the same power source in order to keep your focus on God and what he's calling you to do.

The best example of this kind of unified focus comes from the earthly ministry of Jesus. He didn't choose the most educated, most religious, or most successful people for his team—Jesus chose people willing to give him their all. Christ expects the same from us today. Just as he relied on his heavenly Father, so must we. Through our relationship with Jesus, we have access to God's presence, power, and purpose for our lives.

Regardless of your role or title, your leadership depends on your willingness to rely on him. As Jesus explains in the following passage, everything you do is based on your relationship to God. In order to bear fruit in your ministry, you rely on him. Read through his explanation and underline any words or phrases that jump out at you. Then answer the questions that follow.

[1] "I am the true vine, and my Father is the gardener. [2] He cuts off every branch in me that bears no fruit, while every branch that does bear fruit he prunes so that it will be even more fruitful. [3] You are already clean because of the word I have spoken to you. [4] Remain in me, as I also remain in you. No branch can bear fruit by itself; it must remain in the vine. Neither can you bear fruit unless you remain in me.

[5] "I am the vine; you are the branches. If you remain in me and I in you, you will bear much fruit; apart from me you can do nothing. [6] If you do not remain in me, you are like a branch that is thrown away and withers; such branches are picked up, thrown into the fire and burned. [7] If you remain in me and my words remain in you, ask whatever you wish, and it will be done for you. [8] This is to my Father's glory, that you bear much fruit, showing yourselves to be my disciples."

—John 15:1–8

■ What words and phrases did you underline above? Why do they resonate with you right now?

■ When have you and your ministry been especially fruitful by relying on God and remaining in him? How did your divine focus allow God to work through you to produce spiritual fruit?

■ Now think of a time when you and your team did not rely on God, resulting in withering and pruning results. How did you lose focus in this attempt? What did you learn from this experience about staying focused on what God calls you to do?

■ What are some withering vines that are choking out the fruit of your primary focus? In other words, what activities, efforts, and expenditures are diluting the impact of your divine focus?

_____

They Got *It*

Imagine that you were hosting Jesus at your house for dinner. Naturally, you would want your home to be clean and tidy, the food to be delicious, and the atmosphere to be warm and welcoming. But those details don't happen by accident—they require planning, preparation, and execution. So if you were going to have Jesus come and dine with you, there would be a lot to do, right?

Perhaps that's what a woman named Martha was thinking in anticipation of Jesus visiting the home she shared with her sister, Mary. It's hard to fault her desire for everything to go smoothly in order to enjoy a wonderful meal. And then to have to do it alone while her sister just sat and listened to their guest—she must have felt angry and frustrated. Yet when Martha asks Jesus to intervene, his response reframes her focus—as well as ours.

Read through their exchange and then answer the questions that follow.

[38] As Jesus and his disciples were on their way, he came to a village where a woman named Martha opened her home to him. [39] She had a sister called Mary, who sat at the Lord's feet listening to what he said. [40] But Martha was distracted by all the preparations that had to be made. She came to him and asked, "Lord, don't you care that my sister has left me to do the work by myself? Tell her to help me!"

[41] "Martha, Martha," the Lord answered, "you are worried and upset about many things, [42] but few things are needed—or indeed only one. Mary has chosen what is better, and it will not be taken away from her."

—Luke 10:38–42

_____

- When have you experienced a situation in which you let your preparations distract you from the divine focus at the heart of your efforts? How did you feel at the time?

- Why did Jesus acknowledge the way Martha felt—"You are worried and upset about many things"—before redirecting her focus back to the one essential thing?

- What tasks, responsibilities, and activities are currently pulling you, like Martha, away from the one thing that will not be taken from you? What needs to be cut, shortened, or dropped from your schedule?

- How do you usually handle the Marthas on your team? How can you gently and compassionately, just like Jesus, remind them not to be distracted by that which is not essential?

Factoring *It* In

To have *it*, you'll have to choose not to do everything. Those who attempt to do everything always lose *it*. An Italian proverb says, "Often he who does too much does too little." Too many ministries are doing too little by doing too much. Is yours one of them?

When it comes to divine focus, remember:

- Those who do it all tend to lose *it*.
- The clearer your vision becomes, the easier it is to guard what God calls you to do.
- Instead of saying "and," maybe you need to say "or."
- To be great at a few things and experience *it*, you'll have to say no to many things.
- Innovation requires saying no to a thousand things.
- When focus increases, options decrease.
- Those who have *it* stick with what brings it.
- When you know you're doing a great work, do your best not to get distracted.

With these *it*-factors in mind, spend a few minutes reflecting and praying on how to sharpen and tighten your divine focus. Use the following questions to assist in your reflection and assessment.

- When have you most recently realized you were doing too much and spreading efforts and resources too thin? What did you do once you realized your focus was blurring?

- How many things have you turned down and said no to in the past month? The past week? How many things should you have turned down recently in order to maintain your primary divine focus?

- Do you agree that "innovation means saying no to a thousand things"? Why or why not?

- What are you presently doing that is outside the focus God has called you to fulfill? What must go as soon as possible?

Putting *It* into Action

Spend a few moments in prayer and ask God to guide you back to the heart of your divine focus. Then think about where you are currently in your ministry. Look carefully at the people God has put around you, the resources you have available to you, and the people who are within reach of your ministry, and then answer this question: *What can we be the best in the world at?*

———————————————————

■ Good things are often the enemy of great things. As you narrow in on what great thing you can do, on what God has uniquely equipped and empowered you to do, what good things should you let go?

■ As most churches grow and develop, they usually continue adding more and more (and more) ministries to their organization. Remember, human sprawl is the enemy of divine focus. So now may be a great time to "prune your vines" and return to doing what only your church can do. With this in mind, if you could remove one part of your ministry today, what would it be?

■ What essential ministries are necessary to fulfilling your vision and maintaining focus? If you could do only a few things for the greatest ministry return, what things you would do?

———————————————————————————————

PRINCIPLE #3

Unmistakable Camaraderie

*As **it** goes with the leaders, so **it** goes
with the whole organization.*

Ministries that have *it* enjoy it together. They have an unmistakable camaraderie. Anyone close to them can see it. They can feel it. Affinity, community, sincerity, family. Christianity at its best. The people love being together. And when they are, when the people interact, *it* is electric.

Simply put, the team with *it* love each other. Not only do they minister together; they do life together. What they have is more than friendship. It's something that God gives—a partnership of people with deep love committed to a single mission. You're more than friends. You're a team.

For the church to have *it*, the staff (or volunteers) will likely have it first. As it goes with the leaders, so it goes with the whole organization. To have *it* everywhere, it has to start somewhere. It must begin with your team. As the leader of your team, it begins with you!

You can't fake this kind of bond. Not every ministry team has *it*. Most don't. And its absence is as obvious as its presence in a team.

All too often, people accept and foster independence and self-sufficiency. Not

39

only are they independent, but they're also afraid to open up and be honest with who they are, what they think, and what they feel. With as much relational pain as they endure, especially those who have served in ministry and leadership roles, it's no wonder they're gun-shy.

They're paralyzed with fear, certain that if they let someone in, they'll get hurt—again. As long as you're afraid of intimacy and spiritual partnership, however, you likely won't experience *it*. To have *it*, you have to share it with each other. Just as there's no *I* in *team*, there's no *it* in *independence*.

To be a strong team with *it*, every staff member and volunteer must understand the mission of the organization. This is where vision and camaraderie overlap and enhance each other. Everyone gives respect and credit to one another.

Great teams have real fun together and provide heartfelt, edifying ministry to each other. Fun doesn't require expensive retreats and the latest team-building exercises. Fun is most often a serendipitous by-product of fulfilling a mission with people you love.

Teams with genuine camaraderie are willing to be relationally vulnerable with one another. Teams without camaraderie tend to cover up. Those without *it* can be two-faced. Those with *it* are true-faced. There is no substitute for being transparent and real. People would rather follow a leader who is always real than one who is always right. Others may be impressed with your strengths, but they'll connect with you when you reveal your weaknesses.

Many ministries have victories. But too many wins go by without celebrations. Teams with *it* look for excuses to celebrate. Anniversaries. Completion of significant projects. Ministry launches. Personal victories. Even funny mistakes, missteps, or embarrassing moments can be fun to commemorate.

Teams that have *it* are like family. Part of being family is fighting. Teams that have *it* know how to mix it up good and still be friends. They maintain their identity as a team, loyal to the end. Part of having *it* is knowing that as a group we can have it out and still be friends. Any successful organization knows how to work through conflict. Teams without *it* avoid conflict. Teams with *it* understand that conflict is sometimes necessary to have *it*.

God told Adam that it isn't good to be alone. Solomon said two are better than one. Jesus even said that God is present when two or three gather in his name. Those who have *it* experience it best together.

The apostle Paul says, "You are citizens along with all of God's holy people. You are members of *God's family*. Together, we are his house, built on the foundation of the apostles and the prophets. And the cornerstone is Christ Jesus himself. We are carefully *joined together* in him, becoming a holy temple for the Lord" (Ephesians 2:19–21 NLT, emphasis added).

God wants us to be active members of his family.

We are to be joined together.

God's Word Has *It*

When we lead, serve, and grow together, we each have our unique contributions that work in harmony with everyone else's gifts. Paul famously compared the body of Christ to the human body. The body needs all of the parts functioning together.

A mouth or hand or foot or eye lying on the ground by itself is not just an independent body part—it's useless detached from all the other parts of the whole. Outside of the body, seeking to work on its own, a body part will cease to function.

And it's the same in the church. That's why an independent ministry mindset kills *it*. *It* needs others with *it* to flourish. Read through Paul's descriptive explanation below, and then answer the questions that follow.

[12] Just as a body, though one, has many parts, but all its many parts form one body, so it is with Christ. [13] For we were all baptized by one Spirit so as to form one body—whether Jews or Gentiles, slave or free—and we

were all given the one Spirit to drink. [14] Even so the body is not made up of one part but of many.

[15] Now if the foot should say, "Because I am not a hand, I do not belong to the body," it would not for that reason stop being part of the body. [16] And if the ear should say, "Because I am not an eye, I do not belong to the body," it would not for that reason stop being part of the body. [17] If the whole body were an eye, where would the sense of hearing be? If the whole body were an ear, where would the sense of smell be? [18] But in fact God has placed the parts in the body, every one of them, just as he wanted them to be. [19] If they were all one part, where would the body be? [20] As it is, there are many parts, but one body.

[21] The eye cannot say to the hand, "I don't need you!" And the head cannot say to the feet, "I don't need you!" [22] On the contrary, those parts of the body that seem to be weaker are indispensable, [23] and the parts that we think are less honorable we treat with special honor. And the parts that are unpresentable are treated with special modesty, [24] while our presentable parts need no special treatment. But God has put the body together, giving greater honor to the parts that lacked it, [25] so that there should be no division in the body, but that its parts should have equal concern for each other. [26] If one part suffers, every part suffers with it; if one part is honored, every part rejoices with it.

[27] Now you are the body of Christ, and each one of you is a part of it. [28] And God has placed in the church first of all apostles, second prophets, third teachers, then miracles, then gifts of healing, of helping, of guidance, and of different kinds of tongues. [29] Are all apostles? Are all prophets? Are all teachers? Do all work miracles? [30] Do all have gifts of healing? Do all speak in tongues? Do all interpret? [31] Now eagerly desire the greater gifts.

—1 Corinthians 12:12–31

- The early church to whom Paul addressed this passage was composed of people from various backgrounds, both Jews and Gentiles, rich and poor, merchant and beggar, slave and free. What are the various kinds of people making up your church or organization? List them below using whatever descriptors or demographics come to mind.

- According to Paul here, what happens when one body part tries to detach itself from the rest of the body? When have you experienced a similar issue with your team?

- Based on how Paul explains his metaphor, what happens when one body part envies another and tries to perform its function? How have you seen this occur in your ministry?

■ With your own ministry team in mind, write down each person (or department/group, depending on the size of your team) and how they serve the body.

Person or group:

How they serve the body:

Person or group:

How they serve the body:

Person or group:

How they serve the body:

Person or group:

How they serve the body:

Person or group:

How they serve the body:

They Got *It*

When you think about the intimacy of a ministry group, the bond experienced by Jesus with his disciples is beyond compare. By choosing to pour himself into these twelve men, Christ exemplified how to do ministry—by starting with a core team who gets it. The dozen people hand-picked by the Son of God to accompany him during his time of public ministry had no special training or prior experience. They left behind their former jobs and responsibilities and went all in.

Not only did the disciples recognize the promised Messiah and see him in action, but they also experienced firsthand his love, compassion, strength, honesty, and devotion to them. Nowhere is this more evident than when their Master humbled himself to perform a personal service to each of them. Read through John's account of this special gift, and then answer the questions below.

[1] It was just before the Passover Festival. Jesus knew that the hour had come for him to leave this world and go to the Father. Having loved his own who were in the world, he loved them to the end.

[2] The evening meal was in progress, and the devil had already prompted Judas, the son of Simon Iscariot, to betray Jesus. [3] Jesus knew that the Father had put all things under his power, and that he had come from God and was returning to God; [4] so he got up from the meal, took off his outer

clothing, and wrapped a towel around his waist. [5] After that, he poured water into a basin and began to wash his disciples' feet, drying them with the towel that was wrapped around him.

[6] He came to Simon Peter, who said to him, "Lord, are you going to wash my feet?"

[7] Jesus replied, "You do not realize now what I am doing, but later you will understand."

[8] "No," said Peter, "you shall never wash my feet."

Jesus answered, "Unless I wash you, you have no part with me."

[9] "Then, Lord," Simon Peter replied, "not just my feet but my hands and my head as well!"

[10] Jesus answered, "Those who have had a bath need only to wash their feet; their whole body is clean. And you are clean, though not every one of you." [11] For he knew who was going to betray him, and that was why he said not every one was clean.

[12] When he had finished washing their feet, he put on his clothes and returned to his place. "Do you understand what I have done for you?" he asked them. [13] "You call me 'Teacher' and 'Lord,' and rightly so, for that is what I am. [14] Now that I, your Lord and Teacher, have washed your feet, you also should wash one another's feet. [15] I have set you an example that you should do as I have done for you. [16] Very truly I tell you, no servant is greater than his master, nor is a messenger greater than the one who sent him. [17] Now that you know these things, you will be blessed if you do them.

—John 13:1–17

- Why did Jesus choose to perform such a humbling act of service right before his death? What is the significance of his timing?

- You don't necessarily need to have washed their feet, but when was the last time you served your team members in an equally humble and sacrificial way?

- What does it mean that "no servant is greater than his master"? How does your leadership style reflect the servanthood of Christ?

- What are some bonding and camaraderie-building activities you can initiate with your ministry team this week? How can anything you do together draw your team closer together?

Factoring *It* In

Friendships matter. Studies reveal just how important friendships at work are to *it*. Happier people make better team members. They not only enjoy being together— they look forward to those times. Laughter seasons their gatherings, and mutual respect and sincere caring flavor every interaction. They're comfortable enough to know and accept one another—and love one another—in virtually every setting. This includes in each other's homes.

The importance of relationships isn't simply the conclusion of studies made by workplace experts. Jesus told his followers, "By this everyone will know that you are my disciples, if you love one another" (John 13:35). The people you lead need to see that you don't just believe this as an abstract theological tenet—they need to feel it as you interact with them day in and day out.

When it comes to camaraderie, remember:

- People on teams that have *it* enjoy it together.
- As long as you're afraid of intimacy and spiritual partnership, you likely won't experience *it*.
- God is calling us to more than just a personal relationship with Jesus. He wants us to experience a *shared* relationship with him.
- Those who don't have *it* compete with one another. Those with *it* complete one another.
- We need to take time to celebrate our wins together.
- To have *it*, you have to share it with each other. *It* dies when it is alone.
- Leaders with *it* understand the big picture, have fun, get vulnerable, celebrate the wins, and fight behind closed doors.

- As you look over this list of *it*-factors for camaraderie, which ones stand out to you as areas for improvement on your team? Which ones do you already practice regularly?

- What do you and your team do to have fun together? When was the last time you made fun a priority in a meeting, gathering, or fellowship time?

- How do you celebrate your ministry's wins as a team? What's a win you can celebrate together in the next week?

- How would you describe the way your team usually handles internal conflicts? What needs to change in order to disagree with one another while maintaining team loyalty and cohesion?

Putting *It* into Action

Relationships require constant, deliberate investment. It's great when everyone likes one another and seems to get along. It's even better when they enjoy and respect each other in pursuit of shared ministry goals. But even the best teams require work and intentional development if they are to remain healthy, grow with the ministry, and experience the power of God's presence in their efforts.

Camaraderie can also seem like something that's beyond one person's control—and it is. But whatever your role as a leader may be, others are watching you and learning by your example. Whatever you really think and feel and believe about them comes through, no matter how hard you may try to disguise or sugarcoat your attitudes about them. So perhaps the place to start is with a basic inventory to assess your team's health. You should complete this kind of assessment along with everyone on your team. It doesn't have to be a formal questionnaire or expensive testing service. It does, however, need to be open, honest, candid, and constructive.

Use the following questions to get you started and then decide how to invite your team members to weigh in. Spend some time in prayer both as their leader and then together as a team.

———————————————————

■   On a scale of 1 to 10, with 1 being "very independent" and 10 being "totally interdependent," how would you rate your team today? What factors come to mind that influence the score you're giving?

■ What are three specific ways you regularly, daily even, cultivate camaraderie on your team?

1.

2.

3.

■ How would the people served by your team describe the way you function together? Write down your response below and then text, call, or email three trusted individuals from your congregation or constituency and ask for their honest feedback.

■ What are the greatest obstacles to your team growing closer and experiencing more of *it* in order to be more effective in ministry? What obstacles have you already overcome in order to grow stronger? What obstacles need to be addressed before they grow into bigger problems?

_____

Innovative Minds

If you are ready for change, you are ready for growth.

If what your church or ministry is doing now is effective and changing lives, enjoy it while it lasts. Because what's working now won't work in the future. While the message we preach must never change, how we communicate it must change as the world changes.

This reality may sound discouraging, but it's true. If you don't change, you won't last. If you don't adapt how you share the gospel, your effectiveness will likely lessen over time because the world is changing too fast. You only have to think back on the ways church has been done over the past few decades to realize that it evolves as our culture changes. Again, the truth of the gospel and God's Word never changes—but how you present the message needs to fit the people you serve.

Paul experienced this necessity while in Rome. He realized that the way he preached in Ephesus or Corinth wasn't necessarily the way he should preach to reach the Romans. So he looked for a way to connect with his audience and found it. Paul saw an opportunity to innovate his presentation and went for it: "So Paul, standing before the council, addressed them as follows: 'Men of Athens, I notice that you are very religious in every way, for as I was walking along I saw your many shrines. And one of your altars had this inscription on it: "To an Unknown God." This God, whom you worship without knowing, is the one I'm telling you about'" (Acts 17:22–23 NLT).

In case you think you're not innovative, just consider what it really means. Innovation is different from creativity. Creativity is thinking up new ideas. People with new ideas are not necessarily innovators. People who *carry out* new ideas are innovators. It's easy to come up with all kinds of new ideas and talk about them at every meeting. But trying them out, seeing what works and learning from what doesn't work—that's the way creative solutions come to life.

Innovation cannot be ignored if you want to grow. Accepting this mindset changes how you see problems. When you think about it, every innovation is really a solution to a problem. Too often, teams work hard to prevent problems or come up with easy-but-temporary solutions. But problems aren't things to be feared; they're opportunities to embrace. In fact, many great innovations are solutions to a problem people did not even know they had.

If you're facing a problem in your ministry today, try to think of it as an opportunity for innovation. You might have lost a key staff member, can't find the right facility, or struggle to stream online. What if you reframed this problem into a chance to try something new? What if you told yourself this is not just a problem to solve, but an opportunity to seize?

Rather than recognizing the potential for innovation within each problem, it's easier to stall and blame lack of resources, circumstances beyond your control, and decisions by other people. But what if your limitations could inspire your creativity to achieve your goal another way? God might even guide you to see something you normally would have missed if you had the "obvious solution" or abundant resources.

Whenever you're tempted to whine about what you don't have, remember that God has given you everything you need to do everything he wants you to do. Peter wrote, "Everything that goes into a life of pleasing God has been miraculously given to us by getting to know, personally and intimately, the One who invited us to God" (2 Peter 1:3 MSG). If you don't have something you *think* you need, maybe it's because God wants you to see something you've never seen. Those with *it* recognize that God brings *it*. *It* is not found in the things the eye can see.

Innovation is more about mindset than money. If you believe you can't, you can't. If you believe you can find a way, you probably will. If you think you lack what you need to do what you need to do, you won't do what you need to do even if you have what you need.

Having more is not always better. It can be worse. Why? More people can slow things down. More time can make you lazy. More money can train you to buy solutions rather than create them. When you look at the business world, you see this reality. Most innovative companies are startups that don't have much or mature organizations that enforce artificial restraints to push innovation. So try thinking about innovation as a good thing. Toward that goal, use this concise formula:

$$\frac{Problem}{to\ Solve} + \frac{Limited}{Resources} + \frac{Increasing}{Passion} = \frac{Exponential}{Innovation}$$

Your greatest ministry innovation could come from your greatest limitation—*if* you have a sincere passion to reach and care for people. When you ask God for eyes to see, you may see what has always been there but you have never noticed before. Have you ever bought a car, and then as you drove it around noticed dozens of other people driving the same car? They were all around you last week; you just didn't have the mindset to see them. Limitations and passion have a way of changing our minds and our eyes.

What obstacles are you facing? Ask God for breakthrough thinking.

Don't think about small changes.

Think radically.

Think out of the box.

And then destroy the box!

God's Word Has *It*

When you don't have what you think you need, you often overlook what you actually do have. Many times our own assumptions and expectations get in the way of using the resources God has given us. Instead of focusing on what we lack, we must learn to innovate with what we have.

We see a great example of this in Acts 3. Peter and John were traveling to their afternoon temple prayer meeting when they saw a man being carried to his begging post. He had been crippled his whole life. The beggar apparently recognized Peter and held out his cup, hoping to get some change to buy food.

Which is when God began using Peter's limitations—what Peter *didn't* have—to guide him into giving the man much more than his next meal. If Peter had given money, it might have been easy to smile politely, drop some coins, and keep going to his destination. Because he did not have what the man *wanted*, however, Peter was able to give the man what he *needed*. Read through their encounter below and the answer the questions that follow.

[1] One day Peter and John were going up to the temple at the time of prayer—at three in the afternoon. [2] Now a man who was lame from birth was being carried to the temple gate called Beautiful, where he was put every day to beg from those going into the temple courts. [3] When he saw Peter and John about to enter, he asked them for money. [4] Peter looked straight at him, as did John. Then Peter said, "Look at us!" [5] So the man gave them his attention, expecting to get something from them.

[6] Then Peter said, "Silver or gold I do not have, but what I do have I

give you. In the name of Jesus Christ of Nazareth, walk." [7] Taking him by the right hand, he helped him up, and instantly the man's feet and ankles became strong. [8] He jumped to his feet and began to walk. Then he went with them into the temple courts, walking and jumping, and praising God. [9] When all the people saw him walking and praising God, [10] they recognized him as the same man who used to sit begging at the temple gate called Beautiful, and they were filled with wonder and amazement at what had happened to him.

—Acts 3:1–10

■ Notice that instead of dodging the lame man's attention, Peter said, "Look at us!" Why did Peter embrace this opportunity when he knew he didn't have what the man expected?

■ How often are you inclined to give your team as well as those you serve what you think they expect rather than what you know they need? How often does pleasing others interfere with your ability to innovate?

- When have you experienced God rewarding your willingness to innovate? How did your attitude shift as you realized he had provided you with everything you really needed?

- What's a current limitation that has frustrated your team's ability to move forward in ministry? How might God be guiding you to go forward in a new direction?

They Got *It*

The old adage about necessity being the mother of invention holds true in ministry as well. So often, when you're determined to find a way forward, you will. The trick is surrendering your usual ways of seeing and doing things. By clearing space for your imagination to work, you open up new possibilities that aren't normal or expected but may, in fact, be better. When you surrender your will to God's will, you discover that he has already provided a way where you once thought it was impossible.

We see this kind of inspired innovation in a dramatic encounter Jesus had with a paralyzed man. As his reputation for healing began to spread, Jesus found that many people sought his help in order to be free of the physical limitations, illnesses, and diseases that held them. Sometimes, however, other obstacles prevented them from the opportunity to experience the Great Physician's healing touch. And in the case of the encounter below, such occasions allowed innovation to shine brightest. Read through the following scene and then answer the questions that follow.

[17] One day Jesus was teaching, and Pharisees and teachers of the law were sitting there. They had come from every village of Galilee and from Judea and Jerusalem. And the power of the Lord was with Jesus to heal the sick. [18] Some men came carrying a paralyzed man on a mat and tried to take him into the house to lay him before Jesus. [19] When they could not find a way to do this because of the crowd, they went up on the roof and lowered him on his mat through the tiles into the middle of the crowd, right in front of Jesus.

[20] When Jesus saw their faith, he said, "Friend, your sins are forgiven."

[21] The Pharisees and the teachers of the law began thinking to themselves, "Who is this fellow who speaks blasphemy? Who can forgive sins but God alone?"

[22] Jesus knew what they were thinking and asked, "Why are you thinking these things in your hearts? [23] Which is easier: to say, 'Your sins are forgiven,' or to say, 'Get up and walk'? [24] But I want you to know that the Son of Man has authority on earth to forgive sins." So he said to the paralyzed man, "I tell you, get up, take your mat and go home." [25] Immediately he stood up in front of them, took what he had been lying on and went home praising God. [26] Everyone was amazed and gave praise to God. They were filled with awe and said, "We have seen remarkable things today."

—Luke 5:17–26

■ The paralyzed man's friends had brought him too far not to meet Jesus, so they found a way where there wasn't one—by turning a roof into a door! When have you been forced to find another way forward because an unexpected obstacle blocked your usual path?

■ Like Peter and John with the lame man they encountered (Acts 3), how did Jesus use this opportunity to give the paralyzed man more than he hoped to receive?

■ Why does Jesus ask the onlookers which is easier, to heal a paralyzed man or to forgive his sins? What point was Christ making in the moment?

■ When has your team innovated a solution only to discover it required even more innovation than you first realized? How does an innovative mindset allow you to experience more of God's power?

Factoring *It* In

Many leaders make excuses for not trying something new. It's easy to maintain status quo by claiming you don't have creative people or enough resources to fulfill a ministry objective. Eventually, though, God often turns our excuses into opportunities to strengthen our faith. Like all the other ingredients required to get *it* and keep it, innovation requires regular practice. Learning to see problems, obstacles, and limitations as opportunities is foundational to innovative solutions.

Remember, when it comes to innovation:

- Leaders with *it* do more than just think of new ideas; they actually do the new ideas.
- Innovation is more about mindset than money.
- God often guides by what he *doesn't* provide.
- Problems are opportunities in disguise.
- A Problem to Solve + Increasing Passion + Limited Resources = Exponential Innovation
- You have everything you need to do what God wants you to do.
- Innovative leaders do anything short of sin to reach the lost.
- "All it takes is one idea to solve an impossible problem" (Robert Schuller).
- Innovation is awesome, but don't put your faith in it. Keep your faith in Christ.

■ What are the current limitations you and your team face? How has God guided you by what he hasn't provided?

■ What are three problems, blocked goals, or seemingly impossible dreams that your team could tackle right now through innovation?

Problem #1

Problem #2

Problem #3

■ When was the last time you and your team attempted something that didn't work out as planned? What can you learn to do differently from this experience?

- What experiences, conversations, and events have shaped your ability to innovate? Consider those that have had a negative, inhibitive impact as well as those that resulted in a positive, can-do attitude.

Negative Experiences   Positive Experiences

Putting *It* into Action

As you can see, innovation is a mindset more than a method. Your willingness to remain open and creative when problems occur, as they always do, often determines your ability to innovate successfully. In many cases innovation is underutilized in ministry. Some people always focus only on what they've seen and experienced before. Others are limited by criticism and embarrassment from past failures. A few simply allow their fear of failure to restrain their imagination.

In order to lead like it matters, however, your team must welcome innovation as essential to the ministry God has called you to do. Remember, he has already given you everything you need. He wouldn't guide you to minister the way you're called if he hadn't already equipped and empowered you. What God hasn't provided often reveals how to proceed as much as what he does provide.

Spend a few minutes in prayer and ask the Holy Spirit to free your thinking and to inspire your imagination. Then answer the following questions before implementing what used to seem impossible.

_____

■ If you knew you couldn't fail, what would you want your team to attempt? Why? What's been holding you back from even trying so far?

■ What off-the-wall idea or crazy notion has been simmering inside you? Is there something new God is calling you to do that may seem strange or uncomfortable at first but ultimately change lives and advance his kingdom?

■ Based on your responses to the two previous questions, identify one obstacle, problem, or limitation currently holding back your ministry. As concisely and accurately as possible, write it below:

- Now, set your phone or another timer for five minutes and get ready to brainstorm. Turn off the practical, critical, logical voices inside that usually edit, censor, and prevent you from suggesting solutions. Rule nothing out because everything has potential. Nothing is silly, impossible, or a stupid idea. Okay, get ready, get set, and go!

Now that you've brainstormed, look over your ideas. Choose three of them to share with your team this week. Use this same exercise with them in order to brainstorm even more potential innovations. Spend some time praying as a team before choosing one of these innovations to implement.

PRINCIPLE #5

Willingness to Fall Short

No one enjoys failing, but when those with **it**
fail, they think in terms of failing forward.

Faith in a big God will lead you to take some big risks.
But risks are, well, *risky*. You could fail. Fall flat on your face. Embarrass yourself and the team or even the whole church. But here's the thing: *You cannot play it safe and please God*!

The fifth leadership principle for a church that has *it* and lasts is a willingness to fall short. If you look at any church that has *it*, you will see a church that's failed after many faith-filled attempts. Most of them have failed *often*. These churches are generally led by aggressive, do-what-it-takes, thick-skinned people who are willing to make mistakes. They know that without faith it is impossible to please God. They understand that faith often requires risk.

In contrast, the ministries without *it* are usually the ones playing it safe, doing only what is sure to succeed. They retreat in fear, never having the faith to walk into something new and unknown. As counterintuitive as it sounds, failing can often help a ministry experience *it*. Being overly cautious can kill *it*. On the surface, these ideas don't seem to make sense. But they're true.

Aggressive leaders with *it* are often dreaming, experimenting, and testing the limits. They don't know what can't be done and are willing to try things others think impossible. Because they know they are more than conquerors through him who loves us, these passionate spiritual entrepreneurs take risks. They are not always successful, failing often. But when they do fail, they tend to rebound quickly. Temporary failures are often followed by lasting success. They try, fail, learn, adjust, and try again.

After a series of accidental learning experiences, these hard-hitting leaders often stumble onto innovative ministry ideas they never would have discovered without taking a big risk. They take risks not only because they may succeed, but also because when they fail, they *fail forward*.

In the church world, it's easy to stay where you enjoy the greatest success. You think, *Why take unnecessary risks when this is working so well?* But here's the thing: *Ministry is inherently risky!* You'll likely make some mistakes, fail, and struggle. That's scary, so most stick with what they know. They stay in their comfort zone, where they feel like they know what to do, what to expect, and how to keep *it.*

Only, playing it safe usually leads to losing *it.*

To keep *it*, you will have to go through some failures—probably a lot of them. Disheartened by setbacks and frustrated by failures, you understandably may pull back and resist risking much. You may even begin avoiding risks altogether. Instead, you slide back into a place of mastery, where you feel validated and safe. Only, when you stop risking, you stop growing. And when you stop growing, you lose *it.*

Because the leaders with *it* push through the failures. They know setbacks can be setups for better things to come. They study their failures and learn from them. No one enjoys failing, but when those with *it* fail, they think in terms of failing forward.

Those who have *it* usually grow to understand: *Failure is a necessary part of success.* While great leaders are generally innovative, they are also often scared.

But that doesn't stop them. They know the path to your greatest potential is often straight through your greatest fear. Those who swing hard will strike out often. But they will also knock some out of the park.

As you seek God and he ignites *it* in your heart, let him lead you to the edge of safety, comfort, and mastery. Let him lead you out of your comfort zone and into something that stretches your faith. Something that causes you to rely on him more than ever. Maybe he already has. If God hasn't yet, he will soon. And when that happens, the enemy will see an opportunity to activate fear.

Why? Because one of the devil's greatest tools is fear.

But once you fear something and push through it, you realize you can do what's required despite feeling afraid. You discover that God is there with you no matter what happens. You don't have to let fear paralyze you from moving forward.

The same is true with failure. Once you fail and realize that failing is not the end of the world, you're not as afraid to fail again. You learn something to apply to your next innovation. You realize how God is equipping you for something new. You glimpse where he wants to lead you next.

If you don't have *it*, maybe you need to try something new—and fail at it. Because if you're not failing, then you're not dreaming. When you're not dreaming, you stop learning and growing. God has given you the gift of the freedom to fail forward.

Those who have *it* fail often.

God's Word Has *It*

If you're waiting for your venture to have guaranteed success, you will probably be waiting for the rest of your life. Sometimes the fruit of your steps of faith is measured not so much by what God does *through* you as by what God does *in* you. Sometimes he may want you to risk more in order to trust him more.

God may also want you to risk—even if you fail—in order to cultivate the abilities, gifts, and talents that he has placed in you. Because the greater failure is never to have risked at all. At least, that conclusion emerges from a familiar parable that Jesus shared with his followers. In this parable a master, just before going away, entrusts his wealth to his three servants. When he returns, his response to what they did with what he had entrusted to them is very revealing.

Read through this parable below and then answer the questions that follow.

[14] "Again, it will be like a man going on a journey, who called his servants and entrusted his wealth to them. [15] To one he gave five bags of gold, to another two bags, and to another one bag, each according to his ability. Then he went on his journey. [16] The man who had received five bags of gold went at once and put his money to work and gained five bags more. [17] So also, the one with two bags of gold gained two more. [18] But the man who had received one bag went off, dug a hole in the ground and hid his master's money.

[19] "After a long time the master of those servants returned and settled accounts with them. [20] The man who had received five bags of gold brought the other five. 'Master,' he said, 'you entrusted me with five bags of gold. See, I have gained five more.'

[21] "His master replied, 'Well done, good and faithful servant! You have been faithful with a few things; I will put you in charge of many things. Come and share your master's happiness!'

[22] "The man with two bags of gold also came. 'Master,' he said, 'you entrusted me with two bags of gold; see, I have gained two more.'

[23] "His master replied, 'Well done, good and faithful servant! You have been faithful with a few things; I will put you in charge of many things. Come and share your master's happiness!'

[24] "Then the man who had received one bag of gold came. 'Master,' he

said, 'I knew that you are a hard man, harvesting where you have not sown and gathering where you have not scattered seed. [25] So I was afraid and went out and hid your gold in the ground. See, here is what belongs to you.'

[26] "His master replied, 'You wicked, lazy servant! So you knew that I harvest where I have not sown and gather where I have not scattered seed? [27] Well then, you should have put my money on deposit with the bankers, so that when I returned I would have received it back with interest.

[28] "'So take the bag of gold from him and give it to the one who has ten bags. [29] For whoever has will be given more, and they will have an abundance. Whoever does not have, even what they have will be taken from them. [30] And throw that worthless servant outside, into the darkness, where there will be weeping and gnashing of teeth.'"

—Matthew 25:14–30

_____

■ Based on this parable, how does the master define what it means for his servants to be "faithful"? Is this how you usually define faithful?

■ What fear prevents the third servant from investing his master's wealth? What does his master's response reveal about God's expectations for what he's entrusted to you?

- When has fear prevented you from taking a risk you believed God wanted you to take? What were you afraid might happen, your worst-case scenario, if you took this risk?

- When have you taken a risk you know was worth taking only to see it fail? Looking back, how has God used this experience to help you fail forward?

They Got *It*

Perhaps there's no better case study in the Bible for failing forward than Peter. Time and time again, his education consisted of trying, failing, learning, adjusting, and then trying again. One minute he's brandishing a blade at a soldier during Jesus' arrest in Gethsemane, and then only a few hours later, Peter denies even knowing who Jesus is—not once but three times, just as Christ had warned Peter at the disciples' final meal together.

But Peter's devotion to Jesus was constant despite his failings. And his "failing forward" most likely contributed to God's decision to choose Peter as the guest speaker on the day of Pentecost. Can you imagine anyone preaching with more passion than the guy who was forgiven after denying Jesus three different times?

Peter failed often. He learned from his failures. Then he told people to repent of their sins and call on Jesus, and he led three thousand people to Christ and helped birth the church. Peter failed often. But he still had *it*.

One incident illustrates Peter's willingness to risk and demonstrates both his reward and the subsequent failure of allowing his fears to sink his courage. When you lead on the edge, you learn to face your fears and conquer them, only to have new ones emerge. You learn that the illusion of security evaporates with your last accomplishment. But like Peter, you'll recognize you're safer when you're out of the boat and *with Jesus* than if your fears keep you in the boat.

Read through this memorable scene below and imagine you're in Peter's place. Use the questions that follow to help you think through how God is calling you to step out of the boat.

[22] Immediately Jesus made the disciples get into the boat and go on ahead of him to the other side, while he dismissed the crowd. [23] After he had dismissed them, he went up on a mountainside by himself to pray. Later that night, he was there alone, [24] and the boat was already a considerable distance from land, buffeted by the waves because the wind was against it.

[25] Shortly before dawn Jesus went out to them, walking on the lake. [26] When the disciples saw him walking on the lake, they were terrified. "It's a ghost," they said, and cried out in fear.

[27] But Jesus immediately said to them: "Take courage! It is I. Don't be afraid."

[28] "Lord, if it's you," Peter replied, "tell me to come to you on the water."

[29] "Come," he said.

Then Peter got down out of the boat, walked on the water and came toward Jesus. [30] But when he saw the wind, he was afraid and, beginning to sink, cried out, "Lord, save me!"

^{31} Immediately Jesus reached out his hand and caught him. "You of little faith," he said, "why did you doubt?"

^{32} And when they climbed into the boat, the wind died down. ^{33} Then those who were in the boat worshiped him, saying, "Truly you are the Son of God."

—**Matthew 14:22–33**

■ The disciples became frightened because they didn't immediately recognize Jesus. When have you been afraid because you couldn't tell if God was calling you to take a risk?

■ When have you risked big and experienced the thrill of walking on water? What happened after the thrill wore off?

■ When have you taken your eyes away from Jesus and lost sight of your goal? What did you learn from this experience?

■ What risks are you sensing God wants you to take as you step out of the boat of safety? What gives you courage to overcome your fears as you do what you have never done before?

Factoring *It* In

There's no way around it.

You will have to continue to take risks to get *it* and keep it. That means you have to make a choice. For most leaders, their greatest fear is often failure. But their greatest pain is regret. That is why you will have to make some conscious, faith-filled choices. You can avoid risks, minimize the downside, and continue to play it safe. But if you choose this path, you also give up the upside and you will never know what might have been if you had developed the faith to try. Even if you've never taken many risks—especially if you've never taken many risks—it may be time to go for it.

Because, simply put, in order to continue to have *it*, you will have to face your fears or you will likely end up with regrets.

So get out of the boat. Face your fears. Fail. Learn. Adjust. Try again.

And watch God do more than you can imagine!

Remember, when it comes to falling short:

- Failure is not an option. It is a *necessity.*
- If you're not failing, you've stopped dreaming. You'll eventually stop learning and you will stop growing. Those who have *it* fail often.

- It is impossible to please God without faith, which means we have to risk.
- Sometimes the fruit of your steps of faith is measured not so much by what God does through you as by what God does in you.
- Failure is often the tuition for success (adapted from Walter Brunell).
- Debrief after you fail so it becomes a learning experience.
- If you're breathing, God's not finished with you.
- If you've failed, you have learned something others haven't and are in the perfect position to try again and succeed.
- Great leaders learn the art of failing forward.
- The pain of regret is often greater than the pain of failure. So get out of the boat.

■ What do you consider your biggest failure in ministry, something you attempted that resulted in disappointing results? What did you take away from this experience—to risk more next time, or to avoid risk when possible?

■ What's your biggest regret regarding a risk you didn't take but now wish you had? How has your perspective changed since that time when you chose not to risk?

WILLINGNESS TO FALL SHORT

■ What's been your greatest leap of faith since you started in this ministry? In other words, when have you stepped out in faith way beyond your own ability and comfort and trusted God for the results?

■ Other than Jesus, whose example in the Bible gives you strength, courage, and determination to overcome your fears? Do you relate to Peter, with his many ups and downs? Or identify more with someone like Paul, who had a dramatic before-and-after encounter with Christ?

Putting *It* into Action

In Jesus' parable of the servants' investments (Matthew 25; Luke 19), those who risked saw an increase and received their master's favor. The one who played it safe lost it all. The point of the parable seems to be that in order to grow—your resources, your abilities, your ministry—you must risk. Otherwise, when you choose not to risk, you bury yourself and your future. Simply put, "Risk your life and get more than you ever dreamed of. Play it safe and end up holding the bag" (Luke 19:26 MSG).

Remember, when you take a step of faith, the fear of failure might creep up on you, as it does with most people. *What if this doesn't work? What will people think?*

What if this bombs? But so what? If you believe God is calling you to do something, then feel the fear and do it anyway.

Let God turn the fear into faith. Instead of becoming a hesitant leader, ask God to make you bold and aggressive. Ask him to help you lead like it matters!

───────────────────────

■ What dream have you buried because you were afraid of failing? What burden has God given you that you've put aside? Pray and ask God if it's time to dig it up, pull it out, and risk big.

■ Out of the following risks, which ones have you taken, regardless of the outcome? Place a check mark next to all that apply.

___ Add a new location

___ An additional mission

___ A new community outreach

___ A nontraditional service

___ An online ministry

___ Additional technology (an app, streaming, etc.)

___ Hiring more staff

___ Hiring someone who seems unqualified or inexperienced on paper

___ Unconventional marketing or promotional tactics

___ Shutting down a struggling ministry

___ Reallocating resources

___ Something else

■ Now which of these risks would you like to try? Which seem like risks God is calling you to take? Go back through the list and place a star next to all these items.

■ Go back and read your answer to the following questions in "Putting *It* into Action" from Session 4. Now, reconsidering the risk involved and how God is leading you after Session 5, how would you answer it?

■ "If you knew you couldn't fail, what would you want your team to attempt? Why? What's been holding you back from even trying so far?"

_____

Hearts Focused Outward

Do whatever it takes to make your ministry a place
that welcomes those who don't know Christ.

If your ministry doesn't have *it* and you want it, then shifting to an outward, evangelistic focus is essential. Examine a church that leads like it matters, and you'll find a virtual obsession with reaching those who don't know Christ. They don't add to their mission. Helping people find new life *is* their mission. A passion to share Christ consumes them in a beautiful way.

Churches without *it* can be so tight, so bonded, so close—to each other—that they unintentionally overlook those they don't know. They are welcoming, warm, and hospitable—to their own. But if you are from the outside or your clothes look different or you have tattoos, you might be ignored or even shunned.

Ministries with *it*, however, remember that Jesus came for outsiders. He came for those who were lost. Broken. Hurting. Disenfranchised. Alone. Overlooked. Poor. Jesus came for those whom religion rejected.

Many churches unknowingly focus inwardly, forgetting those who need Jesus the most. These churches are like a hospital that no longer accepts patients. Or a soup kitchen that no longer feeds hungry people. Those without it are often filled with very sincere, Bible-believing Christians. Unfortunately, they're simply more concerned about themselves than about people who are not yet Christians and don't yet believe the Bible. They love the comfort of their Christian bubble so much they're not willing to follow Jesus as he tries to lead them to become friends with sinners so they can seek and save the lost.

But loving people—all people—is not optional. Loving others is *essential*. The Bible is clear: If you love God, you should love people. If you do not love people, you do not love God. "Anyone who loves is a child of God and knows God. But anyone who does not love does not know God, for God is love. . . . If we don't love people we can see, how can we love God, whom we cannot see?" (1 John 4:7–8, 20 NLT).

We're quite comfortable loving those who are like us, but we're also called to love those who aren't like us, and we are especially called to love those who are far from God.

But honestly, many so-called Christians don't. You don't have to look far to find churches full of people who are insulating themselves from the world, hunkering down, avoiding popular movies and secular music. These inward-looking religious types keep their distance from anyone who drinks beer, cusses after a bad golf swing, smokes anything, has a tattoo, listens to rap music, or wears jeans with holes in them. They judge people who voted differently. They criticize rock stars. They stay away from those with a different color of skin. They stare disapprovingly at purple hair and mohawks. They're afraid of bars, rock concerts, and some social media sites.

Too many believers are avoiding "that kind" of person.

Somehow, they've forgotten Jesus came for that kind of person.

Churches that have *it* care for each other *and* for people who are far from God. Churches and ministries without *it* care more about the sheep inside the fold than the goats outside of the church. But think for a moment. What caused the good shepherd to leave the ninety-nine to pursue the one that was lost? Love. What made the father stand on the front porch, waiting, hoping, and praying that his lost son would return home? Love.

What drove our heavenly Father from heaven to earth? There's no doubt about his motivation: "For God so *loved* the world that he gave his one and only Son, that whoever believes in him shall not perish but have eternal life" (John 3:16, emphasis added). What empowered Jesus to suffer mercilessly, to shed his innocent blood, and to willingly offer his life? Love made him do it.

If you are a leader of your ministry or organization, you need to recognize that, for better or for worse, it reflects you. If you don't care about those far from God, the people you lead are not likely to care either.

You may not even realize the message you're sending to those outside the church. Many churches unintentionally turn their backs on those who need Jesus most. We focus inward. We do our Bible studies. We listen to our favorite Christian music. We watch our Christian shows. We speak our Christian jargon. To those outside our bubble, the message seems clear: You don't belong here.

Churches that have *it* are filled with people who sincerely desire to reach the lost. They won't let any excuses stop them.

Love overcomes the obstacles.

God's Word Has *It*

Struggling to love others, especially those who appear different from us, is nothing new. In fact, when confronted by an expert in the law, Jesus made it clear that loving our neighbors as ourselves is second only to loving God with our entire being. The lawyer followed up with another question, perhaps hoping for a loophole. But then Jesus shared a parable that left little room to dodge loving all people—even those who aren't like us.

Read through the passage below and underline any words or phrases that jump out at you. Then answer the questions that follow.

²⁵ On one occasion an expert in the law stood up to test Jesus. "Teacher," he asked, "what must I do to inherit eternal life?"

²⁶ "What is written in the Law?" he replied. "How do you read it?"

²⁷ He answered, "'Love the Lord your God with all your heart and with all your soul and with all your strength and with all your mind'; and, 'Love your neighbor as yourself.'"

²⁸ "You have answered correctly," Jesus replied. "Do this and you will live."

²⁹ But he wanted to justify himself, so he asked Jesus, "And who is my neighbor?"

³⁰ In reply Jesus said: "A man was going down from Jerusalem to Jericho, when he was attacked by robbers. They stripped him of his clothes, beat him and went away, leaving him half dead. ³¹ A priest happened to be going down the same road, and when he saw the man, he passed by on the other side. ³² So too, a Levite, when he came to the place and saw him, passed by on the other side. ³³ But a Samaritan, as he traveled, came where the man was; and when he saw him, he took pity on him. ³⁴ He went to him and bandaged his wounds, pouring on oil and wine. Then he put the man on his own donkey, brought him to an inn and took care of him. ³⁵ The next day he took out two denarii and gave them to the innkeeper. 'Look after him,' he said, 'and when I return, I will reimburse you for any extra expense you may have.'

³⁶ "Which of these three do you think was a neighbor to the man who fell into the hands of robbers?"

³⁷ The expert in the law replied, "The one who had mercy on him."

Jesus told him, "Go and do likewise."

—Luke 10:25–37

- Notice we're told the lawyer's motive—"He wanted to justify himself"—for asking Jesus who should be considered his neighbor. What are some ways that we justify ourselves for not loving others who are outside the church?

- How have you handled people on your team or in your church who tend to be like the lawyer in this parable, wanting to nail down who they should love? How have you handled your own biases toward others?

- When Jesus asked the expert on law who had been a neighbor to the robbery victim, he answered, "The one who had mercy on him." What does it mean for you and your ministry to have mercy on those who are outsiders?

■ What are some ways your church currently seeks to love and serve those who don't know Jesus? What are some new ways you can go about showing God's love to those outside your congregation?

They Got *It*

Most Christians don't wake up one day and decide, "I really don't care about the lost anymore." Instead, this kind of attitude creeps in over time. After being a Christian for a few years, you may not have a ton in common with non-Christians, so it's tough to develop quality relationships. That's why you have to be deliberate about never losing sight of the lost. If you're struggling with this tendency, ask God to break your heart for those without Christ.

Before long, God will send you someone—maybe many someones—whom you will grow to care about. Your love for them will increase. When that happens, you get *it*, and *it's* almost impossible to turn off. Your passion to pray grows. You start looking for opportunities to shift conversations toward spiritual things. You become ever aware that you are representing Christ. When you have *it*, people tend to want it. Your passion for Jesus and his mission becomes contagious.

As you seek out those who don't know the Lord, be prepared to confront your own biases and prejudices. Our human tendency to draw conclusions about one another is a natural result of social interactions. But sometimes we focus on the ways others are different from us rather than how we are all the same. Remember, God looks at the heart while we tend to look at the outside of a person.

The apostle Paul experienced this kind of rocky reception from the Christian community right after he became a believer, when he was still known as Saul. Read through the following passage and then answer the questions that follow.

> [19] Saul spent several days with the disciples in Damascus. [20] At once he began to preach in the synagogues that Jesus is the Son of God. [21] All those who heard him were astonished and asked, "Isn't he the man who raised havoc in Jerusalem among those who call on this name? And hasn't he come here to take them as prisoners to the chief priests?" [22] Yet Saul grew more and more powerful and baffled the Jews living in Damascus by proving that Jesus is the Messiah.
>
> [23] After many days had gone by, there was a conspiracy among the Jews to kill him, [24] but Saul learned of their plan. Day and night they kept close watch on the city gates in order to kill him. [25] But his followers took him by night and lowered him in a basket through an opening in the wall.
>
> [26] When he came to Jerusalem, he tried to join the disciples, but they were all afraid of him, not believing that he really was a disciple. [27] But Barnabas took him and brought him to the apostles. He told them how Saul on his journey had seen the Lord and that the Lord had spoken to him, and how in Damascus he had preached fearlessly in the name of Jesus. [28] So Saul stayed with them and moved about freely in Jerusalem, speaking boldly in the name of the Lord. [29] He talked and debated with the Hellenistic Jews, but they tried to kill him. [30] When the believers learned of this, they took him down to Caesarea and sent him off to Tarsus.

—Acts 9:19–30

- How had Saul/Paul's previous actions and reputation biased other believers against him? What was required for them to accept him into their community?

- Notice that when Paul tried to join the other followers of Jesus, they were afraid of him. How does fear often keep us from pursuing others who are different from us? What are we usually afraid of?

- What do you think Barnabas saw in Paul that caused him to trust Paul's story and welcome him into the group? What do you look for in others in order to continue pursuing them with God's love?

■ How has God used your past experiences before becoming a Christian to relate to nonbelievers? What common interests and experiences help you connect with those outside your ministry?

Factoring *It* In

To see people come to Christ in your ministry, you'll need to have those who don't know him present. This may seem obvious, but you'd be surprised how often it's overlooked. If people far from God aren't coming to your church, you'll want to identify why. Some reasons could include:

- Your church members don't have relationships with the lost.
- Your people are too embarrassed to bring their friends to your church.
- Your building, your services, or the people in your church are subtly communicating "stay away."

Consider how to do whatever it takes to make your ministry a place that welcomes those who don't know Christ.

Another reason your pursuit of those who need Jesus may be struggling is how the gospel is presented. Some churches preach a message that might be straight from the Bible and what some would call "deep," but they make the assumption that everyone listening is already a Christian. They teach the believer and forget that so many of their listeners have not yet crossed the line of faith. Others are simply "How to have a better life" type of messages. That may be helpful, but don't expect people to be saved. If messages contain more self-help than gospel, people will not hear or embrace the good news.

When Jesus came to earth, he was full of both *grace* and *truth* (see John 1:14). Therefore, we should consider how to welcome people with our comfortable environment and friendliness *and* confront them *lovingly* with truth. If someone doesn't see themselves as a sinner, they will never see their need for a Savior.

Finally, you need real faith. If you don't *really* believe in the power of Christ to change a life, people will know it. The opposite is true as well. If you believe with every fiber in your being that Christ can and will instantly transform a life through the power of his grace, people will sense it, feel it, and will often come to believe it as well.

When you consider the role of evangelism in your ministry, remember:

- When we love deeply, love makes us do things we wouldn't otherwise do.
- To have *it*, we have to care about those who are far from God. Many people don't.
- We need to recognize that our friends desperately need Jesus.
- When our churches look inward instead of outward, we're basically saying to nonbelievers, "We don't care if you go to hell."
- Outreach is a team event, and we each have a part to play.
- Be careful not to blame yourself if someone rejects Christ. If you do, you might be tempted to take credit when someone accepts him.
- Love overcomes any obstacle. We need to be willing to do whatever it takes to reach people who are far from God.
- We need to have the faith to clearly share the gospel story and expect people to respond.

- What's the main way your church pursues those who don't know Jesus? How well has this worked based on the number of those who become new believers?

- When was the last time you've had a lost person in your home? How many meaningful conversations did you have with non-Christians this week?

- When was the last time you talked about your faith with someone far from God? Who are the lost individuals weighing on your heart?

- Who are the nonbelievers you prayed for today? How often does your team hold a prayer meeting just to focus on praying for reaching the lost?

Putting *It* into Action

A great evangelistic ministry should offer both grace and truth, both comfort and confrontation. Most churches tend to tilt toward one more than the other. They either have great facilities, amazing worship, warm welcomes, and tasty snacks or they focus more on outreaches, missions, and cold-call evangelism. In order to get *it*, you usually have to find a way to include both.

If you can make your environment comfortable for the person externally and confrontational and convicting for them internally, they often see their need and invite Jesus into their lives. From there, it's about relationships and how they can learn, grow, and share the same message of grace with other people they know who need it just as much as they did.

Toward this goal of striking a balance between comfort and confrontation, think through the way your ministry does things. Use the following questions to help your assessment as you consider how you might need to improve one or both in order to reach more people with the good news of Jesus Christ.

- On a scale of 1 to 10, with 1 being "not comfortable at all" and 10 being "as comfortable as possible," how do you think nonbelieving visitors would rate your church? Why?

■ Now consider the same thing except focused on "confrontation." On a scale of 1 to 10, how clearly would outsiders visiting your church hear that they need Jesus?

■ What is the current evangelistic temperature of your church—warmer or colder toward the lost? Are you willing to lose some people from your church to reach those without Christ?

■ Is your church focused more outward or inward? What needs to change right away in order to engage with more people who need Jesus? Commit to make one improvement today in how your church balances comfort with confrontation.

_____

Kingdom-Mindedness

If you're looking to find more of it *in your ministry,*
maybe you should look for more ways to give
whatever part of it *you have to others.*

Leaders and ministries that have *it* work together for a cause bigger than anything their respective churches are doing. They know that Christ is at the center of all we do no matter who's doing it. They share a vision for advancing the kingdom of heaven here on earth. Being kingdom-minded is the seventh and final *it*-ingredient for leaders to cultivate.

Simply put, being kingdom-minded means focusing more on God's kingdom than your little corner of it. Rather than being competitive, possessive, and territorial, a kingdom-minded ministry is generous, openhanded, and collaborative.

A kingdom-minded ministry is one whose leaders care more about what God is doing everywhere than what God is doing right here. Kingdom-minded leaders know it's not just about their own ministry. A kingdom-minded ministry is generous and eager to partner with others to get more done for the glory of God.

It's hard to have *it* without desiring for other ministries to succeed. When you have *it*, you know that it doesn't belong to you. *It* belongs to God. He gives it. And since it is his and not yours, you're grateful to have it and willing to share it.

On the other hand, the more possessive and competitive we are, the more divided we become. But ministry is not a competition. It's not a reality TV show in which you're about to be voted off, sent home, or told you can't serve. Remember, the ways you minister are part of something bigger God is doing, not only in your own church, but throughout your area, your region, your country, and your world.

Which is another way of saying it's not about your numbers, whether they be attendance, dollars, or whatever you're counting. *It* is not about *your* student ministry, *your* children's ministry, *your* YouTube presence, *your* church app, *your* new logo or website. And *it* is certainly not about your name. *It* is about Jesus. There's no other name under heaven by which we can be saved and so no other name that *really* matters. *It's* all about him.

We say our church or ministry is not about us. But for many of us, "us" is all we can talk or think about. Not only is our kingdom not of this world, but to build our own is surely one of the grossest sins. But what if we prayed, *God, make me more generous. Expand my heart for others. Make me truly a kingdom-minded leader.*

As pastors and Christian leaders, we should be thrilled when other ministries succeed. You may think you are, but have you noticed how much easier it is to be pumped for those who are growing in *another* town? *Yeah, God! I'm thrilled their ministry in that other state is growing!* But if they're in *my* town, it's easy to feel threatened or competitive. *What? The church down the street is doing well? They must be preaching a feel-good message.*

That attitude is wrong.

It's not only wrong—it's dangerous.

God usually won't let a ministry keep *it* for long if they won't give it away. Keeping it to yourself is a sure way to kill it. Ministries that don't have much of *it* often work hard to guard what little of it they do have. What's funny about *it* is the more you try to hoard it, the less of it you tend to have. The more you're willing to give it away, the more of it God seems to give.

Think what believers could do if we all partnered together. Instead of being jealous, territorial, or easily threatened, what if we became extravagantly generous with our resources, ideas, and ministries?

Be generous with *it*! Find a church that could benefit from what you're doing and adopt them. Whatever you can do, do it. As church leaders, we should continually ask, "What do we have that could benefit the kingdom?" God has given you something valuable, and he doesn't want you burying it—he wants you investing it for his kingdom.

Whenever God blesses your ministry, find a way to partner with others. Ask yourself what you can give away. Whatever he gives you, share it.

God's Word Has *It*

Despite our human tendency to want to possess, own, and compete, God's Word urges us to surrender, share, and give generously. The world around us says to be self-sufficient, independent, and at the front of the pack. But the Bible says to depend on God, serve one another, and that the last shall be first. So remember to focus on the truth of what God says the church should be rather than what everyone around you might want it to be.

Because when we lose focus on sharing the gospel and being the hands and feet of Jesus, it's easy for a church to become human-based instead of God-based. Some churches feel like elite country clubs where only certain people are welcomed and accepted. Others feel more like a rec center, filled with activities and events but without a cohesive focus on Jesus. Some churches seem more like school and a kids' center while others are more like group counseling at a therapist's office.

As you seek to be a more kingdom-minded leader, it's essential to remain grounded in God's Word—otherwise, your church can easily drift and morph into something it's not supposed to be. With this goal in mind, read through the familiar passage below and consider how it can help you clarify and sharpen your ministry's kingdom focus.

[1] If I speak in the tongues of men or of angels, but do not have love, I am only a resounding gong or a clanging cymbal. [2] If I have the gift of prophecy and can fathom all mysteries and all knowledge, and if I have a faith that can move mountains, but do not have love, I am nothing. [3] If I give all I possess to the poor and give over my body to hardship that I may boast, but do not have love, I gain nothing.

[4] Love is patient, love is kind. It does not envy, it does not boast, it is not proud. [5] It does not dishonor others, it is not self-seeking, it is not easily angered, it keeps no record of wrongs. [6] Love does not delight in evil but rejoices with the truth. [7] It always protects, always trusts, always hopes, always perseveres.

[8] Love never fails. But where there are prophecies, they will cease; where there are tongues, they will be stilled; where there is knowledge, it will pass away. [9] For we know in part and we prophesy in part, [10] but when completeness comes, what is in part disappears. [11] When I was a child, I talked like a child, I thought like a child, I reasoned like a child. When I became a man, I put the ways of childhood behind me. [12] For now we see only a reflection as in a mirror; then we shall see face to face. Now I know in part; then I shall know fully, even as I am fully known.

[13] And now these three remain: faith, hope and love. But the greatest of these is love.

—1 Corinthians 13:1–13

- This passage often gets applied to couples, wedding vows, and relationships, but Paul was actually addressing the early church in the city of Corinth. With this in mind, make a brief list of all the qualities a kingdom-based church should include according to Paul.

- How does being anchored by love keep your church from losing sight of God's kingdom?

- When have you seen your ministry style become competitive, possessive, or territorial? What impact did it have on your team and those you serve?

- How have you seen putting God's kingdom first improve your church's ability to fulfill its mission as the body of Christ?

They Got *It*

A self-centered and competitive ministry generally loses *it*. A kingdom-minded ministry seems to attract it. As you become more generous, God will likely increase your impact and reach. As your influence expands, you will likely attract stronger leaders, pastors, and creative ministers. You'll reach more people for Christ and meet the needs of more in your community.

The more of *it* we give away, the more of *it* God gives back. Isn't that exactly what Jesus promised in Luke 6:38? "Give, and it will be given to you. A good measure, pressed down, shaken together and running over, will be poured into your lap. For with the measure you use, it will be measured to you."

Holding on to what God wants us to give away never ends well. When we try to keep what God has given us for ourselves, we almost always lose it. If we try to profit from what God wants us to give away, the results can be disastrous. We get caught in the greed trap, and we're never satisfied. One new building leads to a second one, one new ministry calls for the next, and numbers and dollar amounts are never high enough.

This tendency was a problem in the early church as seen in the passage below. The consequences of this particular couple's sin resulted in death, and they provide a sober warning that holding back what belongs to God for the use of his church can be very dangerous and destroy your ministry.

[1] Now a man named Ananias, together with his wife Sapphira, also sold a piece of property. [2] With his wife's full knowledge he kept back part of the money for himself, but brought the rest and put it at the apostles' feet.

[3] Then Peter said, "Ananias, how is it that Satan has so filled your heart that you have lied to the Holy Spirit and have kept for yourself some of the money you received for the land? [4] Didn't it belong to you before it was

sold? And after it was sold, wasn't the money at your disposal? What made you think of doing such a thing? You have not lied just to human beings but to God."

⁵ When Ananias heard this, he fell down and died. And great fear seized all who heard what had happened. ⁶ Then some young men came forward, wrapped up his body, and carried him out and buried him.

⁷ About three hours later his wife came in, not knowing what had happened. ⁸ Peter asked her, "Tell me, is this the price you and Ananias got for the land?"

"Yes," she said, "that is the price."

⁹ Peter said to her, "How could you conspire to test the Spirit of the Lord? Listen! The feet of the men who buried your husband are at the door, and they will carry you out also."

¹⁰ At that moment she fell down at his feet and died. Then the young men came in and, finding her dead, carried her out and buried her beside her husband.

—Acts 5:1–10

■ What resources of your church tend to be guarded or held more tightly than needed? What motivates this kind of holding back?

■ When has your ministry used all of a certain resource and then watched God replenish it and provide more? What did you take away from this experience?

■ Remember the third servant in the parable Jesus told in Matthew 25 (and Luke 19). How is his choice similar to the one made by Ananias and Sapphira? Why were the consequences of their actions so severe in both cases?

■ From your experience, how does your example of generosity influence your team's decisions about using resources?

Factoring *It* In

If you choose to share *it*, the impact for God's kingdom can be amazing. By having a generous attitude and sharing resources, you automatically help other pastors and leaders do better jobs in ministry. You recognize that you're all working together, so you contribute as much as you can to the kingdom team.

You also develop kingdom partnerships that produce results that your ministry could never achieve on its own. You network and make friends, build bridges, and share best practices—all for the benefit of God's people and the advancement of his kingdom.

By modeling godly stewardship, you extend the use of your resources and materials. For example, if you preach a sermon once, it's used once. If you give it away, it might be used fifty times. If five hundred people attend your church, and you spend five hundred dollars on staff and the use of equipment to make a video, that video's cost is one dollar per person. But if just ten other churches use that same video, and each has 150 members, then you've dramatically reduced the cost to just twenty-five cents per person. Any pastor will tell you that God honors that kind of sensible faithfulness.

Your example of noncompetitive generosity will also encourage others to do the same. As others realize you are for them and not against them, that you're all on God's side together, they begin to let go of their personal agendas and work with you for God's agenda.

When you practice kingdom-mindedness, God will bless your efforts. It might be more creative biblical content and ideas. It could be generous givers or evangelistic leaders. God might send you more people who don't know Christ. The bottom line is that when you give *it*, God gives *it* back to you.

The more you share *it*, the more kingdom unity emerges. The things that divide us become less important. We all share our humanity, our fallenness. When we see others being real about who they are, we are drawn together and more likely to help each other. We also all share a mission, and sharing our resources wars against the "competition" mindset that breaks God's heart.

Only God can see the whole picture. Just as a certain message, a certain song, or a certain turn of phrase can surprise you by catalyzing life change in people, we often don't know what God's trying to do until we take a risk. If we truly believe we are his people, that this is his world, and we trust in him for eternity, what do we really have to lose? It's time to focus on God's kingdom and let go of our limited perspective.

When you think about being kingdom-minded, remember:

- The more possessive and competitive we are, the more divided we become.
- A kingdom-minded ministry is more about what God is doing everywhere than what God is doing right here.
- If you are kingdom-minded, you will speak well of and promote other churches and ministries.
- A kingdom-minded ministry is generous and hungry to partner with others to get more done for the glory of God.
- When you have *it*, you know that it doesn't belong to you. *It* belongs to God. He gives *it*. Since *it* is his and not yours, you're willing to share it.
- The more you try to keep *it*, the less of it you tend to have. The more you are willing to give *it* away, the more of it God seems to give.
- Kingdom-minded churches ask, "What do we have that we can give away?" and "How can we partner with other ministries to grow God's kingdom?"

———————————————

- When has your ministry successfully partnered with another church or ministry for a larger impact that neither could have achieved alone? What prevents you from doing this more often?

■ What's one resource your church currently has plenty of but isn't sharing with other churches or ministries? While there may be good reason for this, at least from a human perspective, with whom can you share this resource in your area?

■ Name a local church or ministry in your area that you admire for their generosity. How could you team with them to achieve even greater results for God's kingdom?

■ When has your church or ministry benefited from the kindness and generosity of other churches? What (or whose) examples have inspired you to be more kingdom-minded?

Putting *It* into Action

It's been said that before we can pray, "Lord, thy kingdom come," we must be willing to pray, "Lord, I let go of my kingdom." In order to get *it* and keep *it*, we must loosen our hold on the resources entrusted to us by giving them away for maximum kingdom impact. Usually, this is a process requiring ongoing daily decisions to be generous, open, and cooperative. It's easy to retreat inward and try to control your church or ministry, but you must depend on God if you want to do the most with what he's given you.

With this goal in mind, read through the following questions before spending some time in prayer. Ask God to show you ways to further his kingdom right where you are with what you have right now.

- When a new church or a similar ministry starts nearby, do you feel more excited or more threatened? How can you train your mind to be focused on the kingdom rather than focused inward on success and ego validation?

- Take an honest look: Is your leadership focused more on building your ministry or on building God's kingdom? What can you do as a leader to become more kingdom-minded?

- What can you do to help other local churches simply through your attitude? How can you promote kingdom unity with your words?

■ Review the following list of resources. Place an X by the ones your ministry is currently sharing or giving away to other churches and ministries. Place an O by the ones that you have available that could be given away. Based on the results, consider which resource you will give away first and who you will give it to.

___ Sermons, including notes, downloads, etc.

___ Nursery supplies and materials

___ Curriculum for children and youth

___ Holiday decorations (Christmas, Easter, etc.)

___ Event materials

___ Outreach ideas

___ People (staff and volunteers)

___ Buildings, offices, spaces

___ Finances

___ Web/blog/internet resources

___ Other tech resources, including people

___ Extra worship leaders

___ Other resources: (specify)

PART 3

WHAT IT MEANS TO GET *IT* BACK AND GUARD IT

*Leaders who have **it** don't just motivate; they inspire.*

You've made it this far.

You know all about the seven ingredients to get *it* and keep it.

You've come a long way on this journey. You've seen how *it*-full ministries have a God-inspired vision and are focused on the things that really matter. You've embraced the truth that with-it people share *it* in a deep and sincere camaraderie. You've seen how ministry innovation has increased because of an increasing passion to share the gospel. You've acknowledged that you won't succeed perfectly at everything and that failing is often a step toward succeeding. You're excited that as God softens your heart to be kingdom-minded and focused outward, he tends to give more of *it*.

Most of all, you've recognized that for your ministry to have *it*, *you* need to have it.

If you don't have *it*, then focus on your relationship with God. That's the epicenter for a ministry that has it. Pray to rekindle the passion, the fire, the purity, the hunger for God. Seek him first above all else. "Love the Lord your God with all your heart and with all your soul and with all your mind and with all your strength" (Mark 12:30).

God's Word Has *It*

Unfortunately, even when you have *it*, you can still lose it if you become comfortable and complacent in your relationship with God. In many ways, comfort is the enemy of faith. Complacency is the poison that pollutes passion. Hebrews 11:6

says, "And without faith it is impossible to please God." Keep in mind how Jesus pleaded with his followers, knowing the time was short, reminding them always to "be on guard! Be alert!" (Mark 13:33).

If you want to get *it* and keep it, then keep asking God to strengthen your faith and stretch you. Being stretched once or twice a year isn't enough. Ask him to stretch you daily so that you have to rely on him constantly. Part of being stretched is believing what God already knows: *You have more in you than you realize. God has put more in you than anyone knows.*

Then pray for God to stretch you some more. Follow his direction and go where his Spirit leads you. In order to keep *it*, you might feel like he's undoing whatever you did to get it. He might direct you to change your leadership style or the way you preach. He might challenge you to go to a developing country and leave behind part of your heart. He might ask you to give like you've never given before. He might lead you to do something your closest friends believe is foolish and impossible. He might introduce you to a new church leader who will rock your comfortable world or maybe to a lost person who desperately needs God.

No matter what it may be, always remain open and let God stretch you.

Toward this goal, read the following passage and answer the questions that follow.

> [4] As you come to him, the living Stone—rejected by humans but chosen by God and precious to him—[5] you also, like living stones, are being built into a spiritual house to be a holy priesthood, offering spiritual sacrifices acceptable to God through Jesus Christ. . . . [9] But you are a chosen people, a royal priesthood, a holy nation, God's special possession, that you may declare the praises of him who called you out of darkness into his wonderful light. [10] Once you were not a people, but now you are the people of God; once you had not received mercy, but now you have received mercy.
>
> **—1 Peter 2:4–5, 9–10**

■ What does it mean for you to be part of "a holy priesthood"? What have you sacrificed in order to lead and serve those in your ministry?

■ Peter noted that Jesus, as the living Stone, was rejected by humans. How have rejection and criticism affected your ability to experience *it* and keep *it* in your ministry?

■ How has God stretched you through the process of completing this workbook? What session or theme has stretched you the most? Why?

■ Has God been leading you into taking a risk that would stretch you more? What next step do you need to take in order to step out in faith?

They Got *It*

Without a doubt, Jesus models servant leadership in ways that perfectly illustrate *it*. He never sinned. Never strayed. Never missed the target. Jesus always lived the will of his Father. He was unwaveringly confident in the One who sent him and would never leave him. He was consistent to the core, always and only about "his Father's business." And he bled the mission. He literally bled it on the cross, shedding his innocent blood to cover our sins.

If you want to follow Jesus' example, to find *it* and keep it, then ask God to break your heart wide open. Expose yourself to something that you know will move you. Don't shrink back. Don't fight your emotions. Don't lay another brick atop your self-made wall of protection. Give in to the heart. Feed the hurt. Let *it* grow. Let it bother you. Invite it to overtake you. Feel the pain that others carry. Let the burden of leadership sink into your bones because you care about people so much. Hold on to the passion you have for everyone to know the goodness and grace and love of God.

God loves to give *it* to broken people.

Some of these sessions may have been painful to read. But often where there's pain, there's something that needs healing. So ask God to heal you so that you may have more of it for his purposes. When God begins stirring you, drawing you closer, speaking to you, go deeper and listen carefully.

In addition to the example of Christ, another powerful example to consider is that of Paul. He encountered Jesus in a dramatic way that transformed Saul the persecutor of believers into Paul the apostle of Jesus willing to suffer beatings, arrests, jail cells, and shipwrecks. Read the passage below in which Paul describes serving the church, and then answer the questions that follow.

[24] Now I rejoice in what I am suffering for you, and I fill up in my flesh what is still lacking in regard to Christ's afflictions, for the sake of his body, which is the church. [25] I have become its servant by the commission God gave

me to present to you the word of God in its fullness—[26] the mystery that has been kept hidden for ages and generations, but is now disclosed to the Lord's people. [27] To them God has chosen to make known among the Gentiles the glorious riches of this mystery, which is Christ in you, the hope of glory.

[28] He is the one we proclaim, admonishing and teaching everyone with all wisdom, so that we may present everyone fully mature in Christ. [29] To this end I strenuously contend with all the energy Christ so powerfully works in me.

—Colossians 1:24–29

■ When you think of sacrificial servant leadership, who are the mentors that have modeled this directly in your life? What have you learned from them about getting *it* and keeping it?

■ When you reflect on your own leadership, what's one vital area you want God to help you develop? What impact would growth in this area have on your ministry?

■ What's currently the greatest struggle in your leadership? Do you tend to battle insecurity or self-absorption more?

■ When was the last time you rejoiced in suffering for your ministry? What is God now calling you to sacrifice?

Factoring *It* In

Even after exploring these seven ingredients, you may feel like *it* remains out of reach. You may see other church leaders who have *it* and long to have the impact they have, build a church like they lead, and reach people others aren't reaching. But it just seems to remain elusive, always on the periphery of your ministry.

That's when you must remember that *it* is always a work of God. Yes, God does it through people. But *it* cannot be packaged, produced with human effort, or purchased for a price. God does it, through people, and God can choose anyone he wants to use for his glory—including you!

When you think about it, almost every pastor's and church leader's goals are basically the same. Goals are good, but goals are *not* the solution. Goals do not determine success—*systems do.* Systems create behaviors. Behaviors become habits. Habits drive outcomes. So, if you want better outcomes, create better systems. Small changes in your systems can create big changes in your outcomes.

As you start intentionally creating the right systems, they become the how that will get you to your what. It might not feel significant at first, but never underestimate what God can do with one small habit. "Do not despise these small beginnings, for the LORD rejoices to see the work begin" (Zechariah 4:10 NLT). Define your goal, implement your system, and watch what God can do.

Remember, the ingredients you just explored in the previous seven sessions aren't *it*.

It is what God does as you put them into practice!

So keep in mind:

- Churches without *it* often think the solution is changing their style—it's not. The issue is not the model; it's a mindset.
- The church must be people focused and Jesus centered. While most Christians would say they are, we need to live it out in our actions and in our teaching.
- We need to have the same patience with people that God has with us.
- We have to help people know they are needed and known.
- *It* is always a work of God. God does it through people, and God can choose anyone he wants to.
- You can position yourself to be a stronger candidate for God to choose.
- Goals do not determine success; systems do.
- Strong systems make good people look great. Weak systems make great people look bad.
- A system is a set of principles or procedures that determine how something is done.
- Healthy systems never happen by accident. Systems create behaviors. Behaviors become habits. Habits drive outcomes.
- Never underestimate how God can start something big through one small habit.
- The ultimate *it* is faithfulness.

- What systems presently exist in your ministry? How well are they meeting the goals they're intended to reach?

- Were most of your ministry's current systems created intentionally or by default and convenience? Are you satisfied with the results they're producing?

- What new system do you need to create to move you toward your goals?

- For that system to come to life, what do you need to do next? Who else needs to do what for this system to work?

Putting *It* into Action

Before moving on from what you've learned in this workbook, consider spending some time with the other leaders and team members in your ministry. You might have *it*, but those you're with might not. God can use you to help them get *it*. So describe what this experience has been like as you've completed each session. Discuss the questions at the end of each chapter. Share your thoughts and frustrations. Brainstorm innovative ideas together and look for ways to share resources with other ministries. Pray together. Take risks together.

Once you do get *it*, never take it for granted. Embrace the power of the Holy Spirit working in you to do more than you can ask or imagine. Read through your responses again and see what stands out now that you see a bigger picture. Ask God to show you your next steps in being the leader he wants you to be. Look for opportunities to take more risks and walk by faith more than ever.

Hold *it* loosely. Remember your Source for it. Give it away.

■ What's your biggest takeaway from this workbook experience? What difference will this takeaway have on the way you lead?

■ Which of your views and beliefs about church and ministry have changed since you began this workbook? Why?

- Do you usually think more about pleasing God or strategizing how to grow your ministry? Do you truly desire his pleasure more than the approval and recognition of others?

Finally, to help you get *it* and keep it, read through the following prayer, a Franciscan benediction, and make it your own:

May God bless you with discomfort at easy answers, half-truths, and superficial relationships, so that you may live deep within your heart.

May God bless you with anger at injustice, oppression, and the exploitation of people, so that you may work for justice, freedom, and peace.

May God bless you with tears to shed for those who suffer from pain, rejection, and starvation, so that you may reach out your hand to comfort them and to turn their pain into joy.

And may God bless you with enough foolishness to believe that you can make a difference in this world, so that you can do what others claim cannot be done.

That's it. Amen.

Leader Guide

This workbook is a companion to *Lead Like It Matters,* and it's designed for both individuals and groups. If you're participating in a group study that has designated you as its leader, thank you for agreeing to serve in this capacity. What you have chosen to do is valuable and will make a great difference in the lives of others.

As the group leader, just think of yourself as the host of a dinner party. Your job is to take care of your guests by managing all the behind-the-scenes details so that when everyone arrives, they can just enjoy time together. Your role is not to answer all the questions or reteach the content—the book, this workbook and the Holy Spirit will do most of that work. Your job is to guide the experience and create an environment where people can process, question, and reflect—not receive more instruction.

Make sure everyone in the group gets a copy of the workbook. This will keep everyone on the same page and help the process run more smoothly. If some group members are unable to purchase the workbook, arrange it so that people can share the resource with other group members. Giving everyone access to all the material will position this study to be as rewarding an experience as possible. Everyone should feel free to write in their workbooks and bring them to group every week.

Setting Up the Group

As the group leader, you'll want to create an environment that encourages sharing and learning. No matter what setting you choose, provide enough comfortable seating for everyone, and if possible, arrange the seats in a semicircle. This will make group interaction and conversation more efficient and natural.

Also, try to get to the meeting site early so you can greet participants as they arrive. Simple refreshments create a welcoming atmosphere and can be a wonderful addition to a group study. Try to take food and pet allergies into account to make your guests as comfortable as possible. You may also want to consider offering childcare to those with children who want to attend. Managing these details up front will make the rest of your group experience flow smoothly and provide a welcoming space in which to engage with the content of *Lead Like It Matters*.

Starting Your Group Time

Once everyone has arrived, it's time to begin the group. Here are some simple tips to make your group time healthy, enjoyable, and effective.

First, consider beginning the meeting with a short prayer, and remind the group members to put their phones on silent. This is a way to make sure you can all be present with one another and with God. Then, give each person one or two minutes to check in before diving into the material. In your first session, participants can introduce themselves and share what they hope to experience in this group study. Beginning with your second session, people may need more time to share their insights from their personal studies and to enjoy getting better acquainted.

As you begin going through the material, invite members to share their experiences and discuss their responses with the group. Usually, you won't answer the discussion questions yourself, but you may need to go first a couple of times and set an example, answering briefly and with a reasonable amount of transparency. You may also want to help participants debrief and process what they're learning as they complete each session individually ahead of each group meeting. Debriefing something like this is a bit different from responding to questions about the material because the content comes from their real lives. Following are the basic experiences that you want the group to reflect on:

- *What was the best part about this week's individual study?*
- *What was the hardest part?*
- *What did I learn about myself?*
- *What did I learn about God?*

Leading the Discussion Time

Encourage all the group members to participate in the discussion, but make sure they know they don't have to do so. As the discussion progresses, you may want to follow up with comments such as, "Tell me more about that," or, "Why did you answer that way?" This will allow the group participants to deepen their reflections and invite meaningful sharing in a nonthreatening way.

While each session in this workbook includes multiple sections, you do not have to go through each section and cover every question or exercise. Feel free to go with the dynamic in the group and skip around if needed to cover all the material more naturally. You can pick and choose questions based on either the needs of your group or how the conversation is flowing. Also, don't be afraid of silence. Offering a question and allowing up to thirty seconds of silence is okay. It allows people space to think about how they want to respond and also gives them time to do so.

As group leader, you are the boundary keeper for your group. Do not let anyone (yourself included) dominate the group time. Keep an eye out for group members who might be tempted to "attack" folks they disagree with or try to "fix" those having struggles. These kinds of behaviors can derail a group's momentum, so they need to be steered in a different direction. Model active listening and encourage everyone in your group to do the same. This will make your group time a safe space and create a positive community.

At the end of each group session, encourage the participants to take just a few minutes to review what they've learned and write down one or two key takeaways. This will help them cement the big ideas in their minds as you close the session. Close your time together with prayer as a group.

Remember to have fun. Spending time with others and growing closer to God is a gift to enjoy and embrace. And get ready for God to change your thinking and change your life.

Thank you again for taking the time to lead your group. You are making a difference in the lives of others and having an impact on the kingdom of God.

Also Available
from Craig Groeschel

Available wherever books are sold.

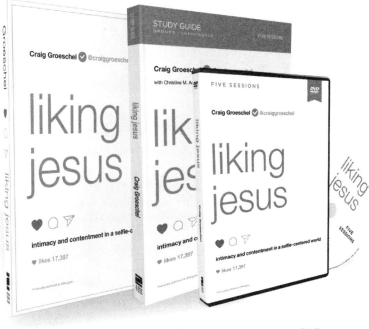

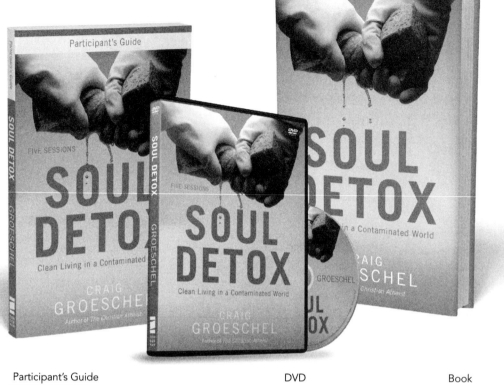

Book	Participant's Guide	DVD
9780310315766	9780310894988	9780310894971

Even though we live in one of the most prosperous places on earth, normal is still living paycheck to paycheck and never getting ahead. Lust and frequent "casual" sex are far more common than purity and a healthy married sex life. And when it comes to God, the many believe, but few practice the teachings of Scripture in their everyday lives.

In this six-session small group Bible study and book, pastor and bestselling author Craig Groeschel shatters 'normal' and turns 'weird' upside down.

Available now at your favorite bookstore,
or streaming video on StudyGateway.com.

Also available from Craig Groeschel

Book
9780310332220

Participant's Guide
9780310329756

DVD
9780310329794

You believe in God, attend church when it's convenient, and you generally treat people with kindness. But, have you surrendered to God completely, living every day depending upon the Holy Spirit?

In this six-session small group Bible study and book, pastor and author Craig Groeschel leads you and your group on a personal journey toward an authentic, God-honoring life. This honest, hard-hitting, and eye-opening look into the ways people believe in God but live as if he doesn't exist is a classic in the making.

Available now at your favorite bookstore,
or streaming video on StudyGateway.com.

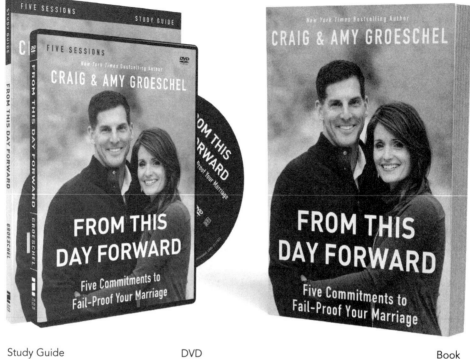

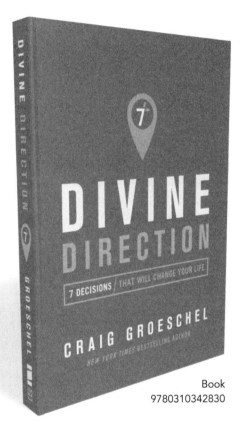

Can God be good when life is not? Rediscover faith in the character, power, and presence of God. Even in the questions. Even in the hurt.

"I want to believe, I want to have hope, but . . ." Pastor and bestselling author Craig Groeschel hears these words often and has asked them himself. We want to know God, feel his presence, and trust that he hears our prayers, but in the midst of great pain, we may wonder if he really cares about us. Even when we have both hope and hurt, sometimes it's the hurt that shouts the loudest.

Book
9780310342953

In *Hope in the Dark*, Groeschel explores the story of the father who brought his demon-possessed son to Jesus, saying, "I believe! Help my unbelief!" In the man's sincere plea, Jesus heard the tension in the man's battle-scarred heart. He healed not only the boy but the father too, driving out the hopelessness that had overtaken him. He can do the same for us today.

As Groeschel shares his pain surrounding the health challenges of his daughter, he acknowledges the questions we may ask in our own deepest pain:

- "Where was God when I was being abused?"
- "Why was my child born with a disability?"
- "Why did the cancer come back?"
- "Why are all my friends married and I'm alone?"

He invites us to wrestle with such questions as we ask God to honor our faith and heal our unbelief. Because in the middle of your profound pain, you long for authentic words of understanding and hope. You long to know that even in overwhelming reality, you can still believe that God is good.

Available now at your favorite bookstore.

ZONDERVAN®

Do you ever wonder, "Why doesn't God answer my prayers?" Do you wish you could see the evidence that prayer changes lives? Are you tired of playing it safe with your faith? In *Dangerous Prayers*, *New York Times* bestselling author Craig Groeschel helps you unlock your greatest potential and tackle your greatest fears by praying stronger, more passionate prayers that lead you into a deeper faith.

Book
9780310343127

Prayer moves the heart of God—but some prayers move him more than others. He wants more for us than a tepid faith and half-hearted routines at the dinner table. He's called you to a life of courage, not comfort.

This book will show you how to pray the prayers that search your soul, break your habits, and send you to pursue the calling God has for you. But be warned: if you're fine with settling for what's easy, or you're OK with staying on the sidelines, this book isn't for you. You'll be challenged. You'll be tested. You'll be moved to take a long, hard look at your heart.

But you'll be inspired, too.

You'll be inspired to pray boldly. To pray powerfully. To pray with fire. You'll see how you can trade ineffective prayers and lukewarm faith for raw, daring prayers that will push you to new levels of passion and fulfillment. You'll discover the secret to overcome fears of loss, rejection, failure, and the unknown and welcome the blessings God has for you on the other side.

You'll gain the courage it takes to pray dangerous prayers.

Available now at your favorite bookstore.

From the Publisher

GREAT STUDIES

ARE EVEN BETTER WHEN THEY'RE SHARED!

Help others find this study:

- Post a review at your favorite online bookseller.

- Post a picture on a social media account and share why you enjoyed it.

- Send a note to a friend who would also love it—or, better yet, go through it with them.

Thanks for helping others grow their faith!